Suck Less at Parenting

How NOT to Raise Little Monsters

Cyndi Lewis

Copyright © 2024 by Cyndi Lewis

No part of this book may be used or reproduced in any manner without written permission from the publisher.

First edition 2024

For My Boys

I love watching you grow up to become little versions of me, and I will always love you unconditionally. Someday I hope that you will understand the choices I have made as your mother and that you will know that I made those choices to give you the best chance at success and happiness in your future. I have set the bar high, my loves, because I want you to reach for the stars. When you catch them, I'll be right there to celebrate your achievements.

… and I hope that I haven't done anything to cause you to need therapy when you grow up.

For My Parents

I could not have chosen better parents than the both of you. Your unconditional love and support have given me the confidence to pursue my dreams. Thank you for never telling me that I "Couldn't". Growing up without the chains of doubt to hold me back, I have been able to believe that I can do anything.

[My children's names were changed to protect their anonymity, but they chose their own pseudonyms: Cabbage (9 and in 4th grade) & Anthony (12 and in 7th grade)]

Contents

Introduction i

Chapter 1: Be More Than You Can Be 1

Chapter 2: Eat or Get Beat 15

Chapter 3: Hello, Routine and Schedule!
Let's Be Best Friends! 31

Chapter 4: There Are No Good Cops or Bad Cops
at the Parenting Police Force 45

Chapter 5: Fight for Your Right to Sleep 65

Chapter 6: How to Behavior Train Your Child 79

Chapter 7: Play Dates Aren't Just for Kids 101

Chapter 8: Think Outside the Tooth Fairy Box .. 113

Chapter 9: It's a Tradition to Have Traditions ... 129

Chapter 10: It's Not Fair That Life Isn't Fair 143

Chapter 11: Stuff is Just Stuff, But Experiences Are the Gravity Bomb!............................. 153

Chapter 12: It's Our Responsibility to Teach Responsibility and Respect 169

Chapter 13: Life Skills 101 189

Chapter 14: Fireside Chats Minus the Fire 209

Chapter 15: Please Use Good Manners and Etiquette. Thank You. 223

Chapter 16: Video Games are the Fast Food of Play Time.. 235

Chapter 17: Parenting Through the Big D – Divorce 255

Chapter 18: The Delicate Dance of the Stepchildren... 269

Chapter 19: When to Yank the Nest Out from Beneath Their Tiny Bird Feet....................... 291

Chapter 20: Be a Good Human............................ 311

Chapter 21: Monsters Be Gone 325

Introduction

It's me, M.O.M. I'm the Manager of Monsters... or I would have been had I not decided to buy a ticket to ride on the Tough Love Train. Let's start at the beginning, though, and rewind to the time before I even started shopping for train tickets to parenthood... cue the harp sounds and blurry transition.

Becoming a parent wasn't something I ever aspired to do. Ask my mom; she'll tell you how shocked she was when I announced that I was pregnant for the first time. "Are you serious?" she asked as she stared at the ultrasound photo in her hand. "I'm not sure if I'm supposed to be happy or not. Was this an oops, or did you plan it?" she continued with a puzzled look on her face. "It was planned, Mom," I reassured her as she allowed herself to smile and exhale. To be fair, I never told her I'd changed my mind or that we had been trying.

I can't pinpoint why motherhood never tugged at my uterus like it did for most other little girls, but it just didn't call me into service. I wasn't drafted into the ranks of motherhood. Maybe it was the fact that I was abandoned on the side of the road as an infant, taken to an orphanage, and then adopted into this country by two of the best parents on the planet. I don't know. Regardless, I just assumed I wasn't born with the mothering gene.

Oh, and babies, they're completely different animals. To this day, I still don't like babies, and I'm very vocal about it because I want there to be a warning in place in case someone decides to bring a baby around and they want everyone to coo over it and fight to hold it. "I just want you to know, I don't like babies, so if someone has one, I won't want to hold it," I inform any pre-glow family, friends, and co-workers. It works. I think I've only ever held three babies: my own two and a nephew that I was guilted into babysitting for the first and last time. I'm good; I got my fill of babies and don't need to hold any others.

Babies are an unsettling nightmare of potential bad surprises for a control freak. I hate surprises. Whenever a baby is present, women's voices go up two octaves, and then everyone talks about how much it looks like one of the parents. It only resembles one of the parents if the dad and baby are bald. How do I know? My sister was adopted from Wisconsin, and when she was a baby, people told her that she looked like my mom. Not possible.

It's hard for someone who doesn't like babies to want to have to have children when they kind of start as babies. I love my kids, but other children, not so much. You know people like me, and you may be one yourself, you're just scared to vocalize it for fear of judgment. I got you. We are out there, but most of us are significantly less in-your-face about it.

I bet at this point, you're wondering what gives me any sort of authority on parenting if I'm so child-averse. When she puts her mind to something, I'm the kind of person who will be amazing at it or not do it at all. About six years into my first marriage, my now ex-husband and

I found ourselves with fewer and fewer friend options because most couples were having kids. Neither of us had wanted any children when we met and married; we were both the youngest in our families, and both sets of parents already had grandkids. Why did they need more from us?

One day, on a long car ride, I decided I was bored and wanted a child. I do that – decide things, announce my decision, and then expect everyone to jump on board immediately.

Oddly enough, my husband and I were on the same page, so the planning commenced immediately. I bought parenting books, read blogs, took handwritten notes, typed up the notes and put them into plastic sleeves in a three-ring binder. I had design boards and budget spreadsheets for a boy and for a girl. But where was the baby?

Part of me had always assumed that if I ever changed my mind about having a child, Karma would get me for saying such mean things about kids and babies. It did. Two months into trying without success I was fed up. Something had to be wrong. Into the doctor's office we charged. "Most couples try for a year before they seek medical help," my doctor told me. "That's most people. I want to know what's wrong now," I said, sneaking a side eye over at my chart on the computer.

"Anxiety" it read on the screen. Well, I guess they're not wrong. Maybe my secret diagnosis would help me get the answers I wanted when I wanted them. A simple blood test later, and my doctor told me I had PCOS. Polycystic Ovarian Syndrome. The first and only piece of my mysterious biological medical history was a fertility disorder. Cue the prescriptions, and two months later, I was pregnant with my first son, Anthony. As soon as we found out the gender, I ordered everything on the spreadsheet and continued my research. I was going to be the best parent that I could be. I hate failure.

Fast forward to twelve years later, and guess what? I am the mother of a nine-year-old son, Cabbage, and a twelve-year-old son, Anthony. Yes, Cabbage was planned; I plan everything. I know I skipped over quite a bit of detail, but hey, this book gives parenting advice first and foremost while my memoir rides in the backseat.

In true form, I have continued to do my absolute best to stick to what I've researched when it comes to the best ways to parent, and by gosh, it's working, even through a divorce. They are super well-behaved, very polite, responsible, and well-groomed, my boys. My sweet little boys.

To add an opposing perspective a touch of humor to my parenting advice and, I will be interviewing my children in the latter half of every chapter. They tell the unfiltered truth, and it's hilarious. And as a way of helping visualize the scenarios or role-playing references, I will again be referencing the fictitious couple, Dick and Jane, from Book 1 (*Suck Less at Love: She Said, He Said Advice on Relationships*). Follow Dick and Jane's story as it rewinds to the time in their marriage before they had children. They struggle through the trials of parenting, but they want to do what's best for their marriage and their child. All they want to do is to find a way to do the least amount of sucking possible at parenting, and if they can help their friends along their journey, all the better.

I hope that my advice, based on experience (and the honest feedback from my children), years of research, and trial and error, will help you, Dick, and Jane find ways to help you work through the challenges and enhance the joys of parenting.

Chapter 1:

Be More Than You Can Be

M.O.M. SAID

No, I'm not calling you to join the military with that chapter title. However, my husband who was an Army Ranger has made many mentions of the fact that I run my house a little militaristically. Calm down; I said, "A little" and "Like". It's not a dictatorship.

He phrases it positively because of how structured and organized my household is run and because of how much he and my kids benefit from strong leadership and structure.

Parenting is about being the best version of yourself every day to set a good example. While it may sound easy, I think it's one of the hardest challenges of parenting. It's why I was always so hesitant to become a parent: I didn't think I could handle the responsibility of being put in charge of someone else's whole life, their future, and whether they would need to see a therapist to undo whatever I had unknowingly done.

I almost wish that for people to become parents, they would be required to take aptitude and personality tests. For parents who want to adopt, the amount of time, money, paperwork, and intrusive interviews are extensive, but people who can have biological children are held to zero accountability. That makes no sense.

Children will emulate and mirror what they see from their biggest role model - you. More specifically, their same-sex parent. To that end, you CANNOT, and I want to stress that again, CANNOT try the "do as I say, not as I do" method of parenting. You will fail 100% of the time. If you act in the opposite way of how you tell your child to, you lose credibility with them, and they lose respect for you. When children lose respect for you, they stop listening, they act out, and the family falls into chaos.

Jane's friend and co-worker, Sandy is at her wit's end. Sandy's youngest son, Jake is causing problems at school, and Sandy just doesn't know what to do. "For shit's sake! The school called again!" Sandy raged as she stomped into Jane's office and plopped down in a chair opposite her friend. "Jake just swore at his teacher. Can you believe that? What was he thinking? He's been such a little monster lately!"

"Good morning to you too, Sandy," Jane laughed as she gave her co-worker a hard time and tried to lighten the mood. "What happened this time?" Jane asked. As Sandy explained what her eight-year-old son had done to get in trouble at that time, Jane stopped her friend. "Sandy, does Jake hear you swear at home?" she asked Sandy. "Yes, but I tell him not to and that he definitely shouldn't do it at school." Sandy snorted.

"Sandy, you can't tell Jake one thing and act in the opposite way. He looks up to you to set an example of what he should be doing. Don't you think it's a little hypocritical of you to expect him not to swear when he hears you doing it?" Jane reasoned. Silence. "I see your point," Sandy agreed. "I guess

I'll have to try harder to set a good example and swear less. Maybe we can work on it together," she considered as they carried on with their "Morning meeting".

The hard truth is that if you don't want your child engaging in some sort of bad behavior, you cannot be engaging in that same behavior. If you are expecting something other than the example you are setting, you're sucking at your parenting expectations. It's not easy, I know, but you chose to become a parent, and it's a huge responsibility. If you don't want to endure the challenge of changing your behavior, don't expect your child to change his.

I'm not perfect: I'm guilty of occasionally dropping an F-bomb or the "S" word. In my house, I struggle the most with the "G" word. Oh my God! That's the one. I find myself constantly correcting myself because I'm trying to teach my kids not to use the Lord's name in vain. They don't seem to grasp the concept of why that's a bad thing to say, and I'll never get through to them unless I can retrain my behavior first. When I catch myself saying any bad words, I try to apologize and say the correct phrase. I'm enrolled in the same learn-on-the-job parenting program you're in, but I am actively trying to suck less right alongside you.

Maybe it's easier to think of parenting as a mentorship program, a big-brother/big-sister type of role. If you've ever mentored anyone (youth or entry-level co-worker), you know that it is your job to set a good, positive example because that person is looking to you to see how things are supposed to be done in life, work, or anything. Mentoring, however, is easier because it's for short periods and in a setting that puts you in the right frame of mind to be the best version of yourself.

Parenting mentorship is much more difficult than mentoring a non-family member a few hours a month. Combine job stress, keeping the house clean, feeding everyone in the house, sleeping, caring for pets, and keeping everyone alive. Then imagine trying to maintain that best-practices-level of mentorship 24/7 along with all those factors, and it's not for the faint of heart. Why do you think there are generations of families who seem to make the same mistake with every subsequent generation, or that sometimes there seem to be branches of the family tree that never produce any good fruit? Perhaps the reason is that they are being a bad example, and the nurture side of the argument is winning in the epic battle of nature versus nurture.

Let's stick with the swearing scenario because it's simple. I love my second husband, Andrew, and he's such a great role model for my boys. He hardly ever swears, and when he gets startled or hurt, he exclaims, "God bless America!" or some other weird non-sweary Andrew-ism. Remember, he's former military and bleeds red, white, and blue. My hubby has found a way to train his brain to steer away from offensive expletives, and I'm proud of him for that. I think he's better at it than I am, dammit! See? He's more mature than I am AGAIN. However, he wasn't always so pious, so his expletive transformation is even more admirable.

What I'm trying to get at is that setting a good example is doable. People are so good at making excuses: "I'm just too exhausted to try to retrain myself," "Why should I have to change? Shouldn't my kid just do what I say because I'm the parent?" No. Excuses will always be excuses, no matter the circumstance. If you want something badly enough, you'll find a way to do it. As parents, we will indefinitely make mistakes and suck here and there, but all we can do together is to try harder to suck less at each hurdle parenting throws our way.

HER KIDS SAID

Mom: Do you know what a role model is?

Anthony: Not exactly.

Cabbage: I forgot.

Anthony: When you say "Role", it kind of sounds like a role to do something...

Mom: Well, that's what it is. A role model is someone you look up to because they're the person you want to be for certain reasons.

Both: Oh yeah.

Mom: So, now that you know that, who do you see as a good role model, and why?

Anthony: Andy.

Mom: Why?

Anthony: Cuz he does a lot of things that you don't tell him to do.

Mom: Like what?

Anthony: Like probably lawn mowing outside or fix stuff for you, and he does over and beyond what you ask him to do.

Cabbage: Andy because he just does it when you ask him to do something, or he just does it when you don't ask, or something like that.

Mom: Have I ever told you not to do something, but then you saw me do it?

Both: Yeah.

Mom: Like what?

Cabbage: (*Raising his hand*) I know! It was liiiike... oh no, I forgot. Anthony – you go.

Mom: What have I told you not to do, and then I did it anyway?

Anthony: This is hard cuz you haven't done a lot of stuff that you said not to do.

Mom: Well, you said "Yes" pretty quickly.

Cabbage: (*Raising his hand*) Ooh, I know, I know, I know!

Mom: What?

Cabbage: You said not to go outside, but then you went outside.

Mom: When would I ever say, "Don't go outside"?

Cabbage: I don't know.

Anthony: When it's like snowing.

Mom: I would never tell you not to go outside. I always want you to go outside. Think of something better than that. (Waits) Anything?

Cabbage: Don't go downstairs because there are presents, but then you go downstairs.

Mom: Okay, these don't count.

Anthony: NO, NO, NO, NO, NO! Maybe... don't go on the treadmill, but then you go on it.

Mom: I'm talking about behavioral things that I'm consistently trying to teach you not to do.

Andrew: (From the other room) Like getting in the water when you're told not to get in the water.

Mom: Yes. Exactly. Like if I said, "Don't jump in that puddle," and then I went and did it, that sort of a thing. Not "Don't step on my treadmill because I don't want you to destroy it"; that's a different thing. Do you have any of those?

Cabbage: Oh yeah... wait, I had it. (*Long pause*) um...

Mom: So, no. Okay. What would happen if I told you not to do something but then did it, like the puddle situation? Would you think it's okay or not okay to do it because you saw me do it?

Anthony: Not okay because you told us not to do it, and you're the adult, and...

Cabbage: Yeah. You can do whatever you want to do.

Mom: Is there anything that I do that you think I shouldn't because it sets a bad example for how you should behave?

Cabbage: Swear.

Mom: I don't swear.

Anthony: Well, you do once in a while.

Cabbage: Don't eat a lot of candy.

Mom: I don't eat a lot of candy.

Anthony: Well, what do you do on your phone, like Instagram and Snapchat?

Mom: I don't use Snapchat.

Cabbage: I forgot. What was the question again?

Mom: The question was, is there anything that I do that I shouldn't because it sets a bad example?

Cabbage: I don't think you do anything wrong because you're a Safety Mom.

Mom: A Safety Mom? (*Anthony starts laughing*) What's a Safety Mom?

Cabbage: Like my friend's mom... she's a Safety Mom, so um. He can only play one video game, and it's called Prodigy (*a math teaching app from school*). That's it.

Mom: So that makes me a Safety Mom? Where did you come up with the term "Safety Mom"?

Cabbage: From my friend.

My littles don't have a lot of examples of "do-as-I-say-not-as-I-do" parenting because I try very hard to set a good example, minus the swearing that I'm still working on. My situation is a little unique in that I am no longer married to their father and am remarried (to a man who will not be moving in with us until he retires in about two-and-a-half more years), but I was very careful in who I chose as a partner after my divorce because I knew that the man that I chose would be another same-sex role model in their lives. Oh yes, dating when you have children is a very complicated puzzle, but we'll delve more deeply into that later.

Regardless of your relationship status, however, parenting is the biggest challenge you will face in life because you are shaping the world for someone else and their whole future. Not only are you responsible for yourself and your actions, but you are also responsible for someone else and his or her actions. It's a lot, I know. It's like a job but so much harder.

Unfortunately, or fortunately for you, how you are is how your children will be. If you excel at something, chances are, your children will also excel at that. Conversely, if you suck at something, your children will suck at that same thing. If you don't want your children to suck as adults, then you need to stop sucking first, but changing your behavior patterns first is not so easily done. Sometimes it takes our children mimicking our mistakes for us to see ourselves more clearly and what we need to change and work on.

Chapter 2:

Eat or Get Beat

M.O.M. SAID

When I was a kid, I don't remember being given options for dinner other than what was being served. Most people my age and older never had the option to complain about or demand something else for dinner; it just wasn't done. In these modern times, a new degree of passiveness in parenting has allowed children to demand their own personal menus. Can you imagine telling your parents that you weren't going to eat what they made? "I only eat buttered noodles, *Mom*." THWAK upside the head! Our parents would never have tolerated that kind of ungrateful, sassy behavior.

Most of us would have received quite a harsh thrashing for that kind of insubordination. It baffles me how often I hear peers tell me that their kids have special eating habits aside from the rest of the family. No, I'm not talking about food allergies, I'm talking about the ridiculousness of parents having to cater to their children like they're tiny royalty. "Here, Prince so-and-so, I made you your favorite dinner again of chocolate-covered bread with a side of candy." Okay, it's not that bad, but it might as well be.

My ex-husband's sister would tell her kids, "Eat or get beat!" No, they didn't get beat, but it was her tongue-in-cheek way of saying that she didn't cater to whims, and those kids eat way more diverse foods than any kids I know. I once witnessed one of them dive into a fish boil (two words that, when put together, make me gag) and pull a fin out of her mouth, "Oh, I guess there are fins in here," she stated with a cavalier attitude as she continued enjoying the bony stew that I found completely repulsive and inedible.

What has shifted in society that children have been able to throw this culinary coup? What happened to eating what you were given and being thankful? I'm pretty sure most of you have been asked the pointed question, "Don't you know there are starving children in other countries who would be happy to have your food?" Have people become so wealthier and time-laden today that they can afford to buy and make two different meals? No! Parents are getting soft, and they're sucking.

> *Dick and Jane had volunteered to babysit Jane's niece for a weekend. Not having had much real-life experience parenting, Dick and Jane were a little clueless when it came to how to manage a four-year-old. "Megan," Jane addressed her sweet little niece, "We are having tater tot hotdish for dinner. Doesn't that sound yummy?" Jane's smile and optimism faded when Megan quickly spat back, "No! I hate that. I want pizza!"*

> *Jane looked at Dick with confusion. "What am I supposed to do now?" she whispered to her husband, who looked as clueless as she felt. "Her mom told me that she should eat whatever we are having; that's what they do at their house," she continued.*

> *"How about you try the tater tot hotdish, and if you don't like it, I will make you some frozen*

pizza?" Jane asked, trying to negotiate a peace treaty with the little monster. "No! That sounds gross. I want pizza!" screamed Megan, getting herself more and more worked up. "Megan, your mom said that you need to eat what we are eating, or you won't get to eat anything," Jane explained. "No!" yelled Megan. "Okay, you still need to sit here with us while we eat. You can choose to eat what I make or not, but there will be no other choices," Jane explained as she did her best to hold fast in the battle of wills.

"HRRUMPH!" Megan pouted with her arms crossed as she sat quietly at the table. "Mmmm... this is so good!" Praised Dick. "It's my favorite. Thanks, honey." The two of them ate their dinner while ignoring the pouting child. Out of the corner of her eye, Jane saw Megan pick up a warm tater tot and sneak it into her mouth. Dick and Jane pretended not to notice as they finished their food, and when Megan had cleaned most of her plate, Jane said, "Thank you so much for trying it. I worked really hard to make it. Did you like it?"

Smiling sheepishly with food still in her mouth, she responded, "Yes. I'm sorry, Auntie Jane. It was really good."

A version of that scenario played out in the early years of my parenthood journey. It works if you can stay strong. When my children were little, I told them that if they didn't want to finish their food or eat what they were given, they wouldn't get a snack, and their next meal would be breakfast. The food philosophy in my house has always been as follows:

It's too bad if you don't like it. I planned the menu, I shopped for the groceries, I paid for the food, I made the food, and I expect you to eat it.

Some of my friends call me heartless, but I have very strong willpower, especially when trying to make a point. I suppose you could call it stubbornness, but I am 100% sure that my children won't wake up dead if they miss one dinner, so I don't back down. All it takes is one missed meal and an empty stomach overnight to learn a lesson quickly. I will never waive the white dinner napkin flag to my children.

My now nine- and twelve-year-old sons know the rules of food quite clearly, but I still get the occasional pushback, especially when they hear the words "New recipe". I like a challenge, and trying new recipes is one of the ways I find to keep my brain in tip-top shape. The new recipe rule in my house is this:

If I make something new, you still must clean your plate to earn dessert.

The only caveat to the new recipe rule is that if I think it sucks, you don't have to finish it, but you do have to eat at least half of it. I'm not a total monster. Sometimes, recipes do look better on paper.

My other retort to the new recipe grumble is, "If you never tried new things, you would never have found out that your favorite food is Nutella crepes ('chocolate crepes', the kids call them)." They comply once explained in terms near and dear to their little chocolate-coated hearts. They can see the logic now, and it's awesome!

There are also rules in my house about desserts and sweets. If Mommy makes a new dessert, everyone who earns a dessert must choose Mommy's dessert. With desserts of any kind, there are two portion sizes of "treats": lunch treat and dinner treat. Lunch treats can be earned by cleaning one's lunch plate in a timely fashion, and lunch treats are about half the size of dinner treats. For example, when the boys were into Hershey bars as their treat, one row of three rectangles of chocolate was considered a lunch treat. Double that to half of a candy bar, and that's a dinner treat.

And speaking of lunch, I swear that it is every parent's curse that the school will serve the same thing for lunch as you've planned to serve for dinner. Yes, I know that the school has menus, but does anyone look at those? There have been a couple of recent times when I told the kids what was for dinner, and they groaned about it because the school served it for lunch that day, they had it at Dad's the day before, or they just don't like that dish. My response to this kind of insolence and disrespect is, "Whoever complains about what's for super must plan, pay for, and make the next dinner. So, I'll ask you again: What do you have to say about what I'm making for dinner?" The answer always changes after a moment to digest the options.

My boys never eat sweets or candy without asking, always eat what they're served, and obey the house rules of lunch and dinner treats. Of course, there have been times when I had to enforce my own rules and deny any treats, but the lessons to be learned are worth the battles that always ensued. The good news is that once you establish these rules and everyone is on the same page, most food-related arguments are easy to settle.

HER KIDS SAID

Mom: What is your favorite food? Anthony?

Anthony: How about chocolate crepes?

Mom: Cabbage?

Cabbage: Chocolate crepes.

Mom: If how much you liked the taste of food was on a one-to-ten scale, one being something you will throw up if you eat, and ten being your favorite food, how would you rate the school food, Anthony?

Anthony: A six... like a five-to-six because it's not that great.

Mom: I'm pretty sure that you have been taking extra entrees.

Anthony: Yeah, I know, but it's only great those days. Most of the time it's a four.

Mom: A four?!

Anthony: (*Waving his arm*) A five or six.

Mom: Cabbage, what's your rating?

Cabbage: Three, four, or five.

Mom: Can you, like not pick your nose while we're doing this? What about the food at Texas Roadhouse?

Anthony: Steak? It would probably be an eight, but most of the time, it's a nine. (*Gives a thumbs up and smiles*)

Mom: Ooh, that's pretty high. What about you, Cabbage?

Cabbage: Seven or eight.

Mom: What about Culver's?

Anthony: Eight!

Cabbage: Six or seven.

Mom: What about food at Grandma Nancy's?

Anthony: Like your mom? (*Points at me*)

Cabbage: Yes, my mom.

Both: (*Silence*)

Anthony: Seven. Not to be rude, but seven.

Cabbage: Seven.

Mom: What about Mommy's cooking?

Cabbage: Ten, no two hundred out of ten.

Anthony: Nine point five or a ten.

Mom: Nine point five?!

Cabbage: What the heck?

Anthony: I don't like some of the stuff that you make.

Cabbage: Well, I put a ten out of ten.

Mom: You gave me a twelve yesterday.

Cabbage: Yeah, that's true.

Mom: Do you like trying new foods or when Mommy makes a new recipe?

Cabbage: Yes!

Anthony: Not exactly, no. (*Laughs uncomfortably*)

Mom: Why?

Anthony: Well, if I didn't like it, and I would have to eat it... I don't like to eat something that I don't like.

Mom: Most people don't, but how do you know you don't like it if you haven't tried it? When you hear "new recipe", what goes through your mind? What's your first reaction?

Anthony: Oh boy, I'm going to have to try something new, but I don't really want to do it, but I know I'm going to have to anyways.

Mom: That's right. Cabbage – what about you? Do you like the new recipes?

Cabbage: Yes.

Mom: So, when I say, "Hey, we're having a new recipe for dinner, what do you think immediately?

Cabbage: Yay. Can you ask me why I'm excited to eat the new food?

Mom: Why?

Cabbage: Cuz I'm a daredevil.

Mom: Oh, okay. You already had that answer prepared?

Cabbage: Yeah.

Mom: Do you think that kids should get to request that the parents make them something special or different for dinner than what they are eating?

Anthony: Yes and no. If the parent is nice, then yes.

Mom: Oh, so I'm not a nice parent?

Both: You are!

Mom: So, you think it's okay for kids to be like, "I don't want to eat all the things that you made for me, paid for, and did all this stuff..."

Anthony: No! I'm saying that you should do that but get less of it.

Mom: I'm talking about completely separate meals, not different portion sizes.

Anthony: Oh no!!!!

Cabbage: I would never say, "I don't want to eat this."

Anthony: Well, maybe once or twice.

Mom: Why do you think it's not okay for kids to request that they have different food?

Cabbage: Because they are not adults, and adults always make rules.

Anthony: And because then, what was the whole point of getting all that food for nothing? Then it goes down the drain.

Mom: What stops you from going into the candy area and eating what you want, when you want?

Cabbage: Because I would get in super bad trouble, and you would get in trouble with the manager.

Mom: The manager? Who's your manager?!

Cabbage: What did you say?

Mom: I said, "What stops you from going into OUR candy area..."

Cabbage: OH! I'd get in super bad trouble, and I probably wouldn't want candy at that time.

Anthony: Get in trouble, and probably because you'd have diarrhea and a lot of stuff you don't want.

Cabbage: (*Jumping up and down with his arm up*) I know a good one! Because Santa will know.

Mom: That's right, Santa will know. Do you think that having a smaller treat for lunch makes sense, why?

Cabbage: Yes, because we don't have that much food for lunch.

Anthony: And it's only lunch, not dinner because dinner you have way more food, and lunch you only have not that much.

Mom: So, a treat should be proportionate to the amount of food given?

Cabbage: Um hm.

Anthony: Yeah.

Cabbage: And how good you are at lunch.

Mom: That's right.

Food costs have never been so high as they are right now, and that increase has only highlighted the importance of course correcting your children when it comes to everyone eating the same meal. I struggle to afford to feed a family of four even when everyone is eating what I make and cleaning their plates, and I can't imagine making multiple meals or dealing with family members refusing to eat dinner.

Fighting and winning the food battle in the early years will set you up for less resistance from the enemy down the road. The enemy is Le Resistance… not your children. Remember, the family is a unit – a team. Everyone needs to know and play by the same rules to be successful and win the game of life.

It's not all about the money that the food costs, even though part of it is. The food fight is also an issue of respecting the parents and their resources. Parents who can command respect around food will also gain ground in getting overall respect from their children, and eventually, they will reap the reward of the fruits of their labor.

Chapter 3:

Hello, Routine and Schedule! Let's Be Best Friends!

M.O.M. SAID

When people ask me how I can accomplish so much in a day or in my life, my answer is, "Excellent time management." Essentially being a single parent until my husband retires and moves in with me, I have a lot on my plate to manage: my full-time job, shuttling two kids to two different schools, homework, volunteering at two different organizations, running a new small business, cooking homemade dinners, and writing this book series. It's a lot, but being bored makes me anxious, and I'd rather be exhausted and productive than anxious.

Being able to put schedules and routines into place not only helps me run my life like a pro, but it also helps my children to be secure in knowing what's happening, even if they're not in control. Kids often fight their parents regarding things like when to leave for school, when they can have snacks, and how much screen time they can have because children feel like they have no say or control over what or when things happen. That ambiguity will cause them to act out because their behavior and reactions are the only things they can control.

From the moment my children were born, they were born into a schedule. I charted feeding times, naps, poops, everything. From those charts, I created schedules for us and for any caregivers we had, usually nannies or au pairs. Sticking to schedules from the beginning is one thing that helped my children to be great sleepers. Even before children can comprehend what a routine is, they will benefit from it greatly.

As children age, their routines and schedules adjust. When you put schedules in place, and everyone is aware of them and sticks to them, your children will feel settled in knowing what's happening, what's expected, and what the day's timeline is. Routines make people feel safe. It's uncertainty that freaks people out. Let me illustrate what my weekday schedule for the family looks like:

- **4:00 am:** I jump out of bed to exercise and get ready.

- **5:45 am:** Cabbage wakes himself up with his Alexa alarm, and he wakes up Anthony at **6:00 am**.

    o Children get dressed, make beds, feed themselves breakfast, and do their chores.

- **7:10 am:** I yell, "Let's go!" Kids pack up, and we head out the door for school.

- **7:24 am:** I pull into the road where the middle school is. Drop off middle schooler, drive to elementary school, sign in to before-school childcare program, and head to work.

- **7:48 am:** Arrive at the office.

- **2:00 pm:** Leave work to sit in parent-pickup hell at the middle school. Multitask and work from the car until Anthony emerges around **2:49 pm**.

- **3:05 pm:** Get Anthony started on homework.

- **3:45 pm:** Leave the house to retrieve Cabbage from the elementary school after-school program.

- **4:00 pm:** Pick up Cabbage.

- **4:15 pm:** Arrive back home. Kids start and finish homework and take showers while I start dinner.

- **5:00 pm:** Dinner is served (always at 5:00 sharp).

- **6:20 pm:** Snack time for the kids.

- **7:20 pm:** Kids head upstairs to brush their teeth and have a little iPad time in their respective bedrooms.

- **8:00 pm:** I take the iPads and hug the kids goodnight. They can read quietly or color in their rooms before they put themselves to bed. No electronics or high-level of activity are allowed.

Often, I'll give warnings of, "Ten minutes until bedtime", or "We are leaving in a few minutes". Giving them a heads-up on the schedule helps me ward off comments like, "I just want to finish this video" because I can fall back on, "I told you we were leaving soon."

> *Dick and Jane went over to visit their friends who had a two-year-old and a four-year-old. While they were visiting, Jane noticed that the oldest child had emerged with a chocolate fudge pop in her hand and was happily eating it in the living room as the chocolate dripped onto the carpet.*
>
> *"Um, is she supposed to have that?" Jane asked her friend. "Well, no, but she can open the freezer on her own now, and sometimes I even find melted ice cream behind the couch." The take-it-or-leave-it attitude that her friend seemed to have toward the*

fudge-covered behavior was baffling to Jane. Why would she let this bad behavior continue?

"Well, she's probably hungry for a snack so it's fine," Jane's friend continued. "Is it snack time? What do they normally have for a snack?" Probed Jane, carefully trying not to overstep her friend's parenting ethos. "There really isn't a snack time. They kind of just grab things when they're hungry." "Yikes", thought Jane as she made mental notes on what she didn't want to do when she became a parent.

My littles know when snack times are and what the approved snacks are for which time of the day. Having that knowledge allows them the freedom to run their own lives by watching the clock and being able to make their own decisions as to the snack they want. Because they know the parameters around snacking, they know what choices will and won't get them in trouble. It's a great system. When it comes to the after-dinner snack, they will ask me to remind them, "Mommy, would you tell me when it's snack time?" They're tired, I'm tired, but they know if they miss the snack time window, there is no snack, so they plan accordingly.

Children who feel as though they have no control over anything in their lives will lash out in some way or another... some form of bad behavior. Something else that you can do to give your children the illusion of control is to let them pick out their outfits for the day. My children seem to coordinate shirts whenever possible, but unfortunately, they keep choosing the same video game-themed shirts and leaving drawers full of new shirts untouched. Yes, their lack of diversifying their clothing portfolio annoys me, but I understand the value of giving them a choice.

I suppose you could say that I suck at buying too many clothing options knowing that they won't wear them. When their redundant shirt selection starts to bother me, I ask if they would please choose something they haven't worn before because "I'll stop buying you new clothes if you never wear them". They do, for a day or two, but then they go back to the same dumb shirts. This fight in my house isn't WWIII, but yes, I could push them harder to suck less at clothing diversification.

Another great benefit of routines and schedules is that they teach your children the valuable life skill of time management. Having your children on a schedule also helps them to develop good sleep patterns at every stage in their lives. My youngest has learned that if he sleeps past six am on a weekend, he can't get to sleep at bedtime. He has solved his sleep issue by setting his alarm every morning for 5:45 am. I'm so proud of my little mini-me planner!

If you're a planner with a routine and schedule in your life, you can understand how unsettling it might be if you were forced to approach every day without having any knowledge of what was coming next or when. Keeping your children apprised of what is happening and what deterrence from the schedule may be will reduce their anxiety and bad behaviors.

Every fall, I make a calendar for the children for the upcoming year, including custody schedules, no school days, trips, holidays, etc. As soon as that calendar gets into the hands of my youngest, he checks to see where he will be and for which holiday. "Oh good – we are at your house for Halloween!" he has confessed more than once. "When are we going to the cabin?" or "When is vacation?" are questions that can simply be answered with, "Please refer to your calendar."

I know that my level of planning and scheduling is a bit extreme and probably deserves a reality show. However, I do hope that by setting a good example for my children and showing them how routines and schedules can make their lives easier, they will learn and implement that knowledge in their lives going forward.

If you as a parent are not great with scheduling routines, you may want to make more of an effort to suck less at it because it will be beneficial for everyone. Sit down with your children and make a schedule together, and you can keep each other in check while also learning together. What a great lesson to teach your children: You're never too old to learn a new skill or to suck less.

HER KIDS SAID

Mom: Why do you think Mommy can get so many things done in a short amount of time?

Anthony: Because you are organized.

Cabbage: Because you're a neat freak.

Mom: What do you like about the schedule at my house, and what don't you like about it?

Anthony: I like it because on a school day, you don't have to wake up so late and be late for school, but I don't like that we have to do everything every single day of the year until we're like eighteen.

Cabbage: I just like it; I don't know how to explain it.

Mom: You just like the schedule?

Cabbage: Yeah.

Mom: There's nothing you don't like about the schedule?

Cabbage: Wait... (*Pauses*) No, there's nothing I don't like about it. It's organized.

Mom: Do you use your calendars, the ones I make that show you whose house you're going to be at, and how would you feel if you didn't have them to know what's ahead in the coming weeks and months?

Cabbage: It's awesome to have it because like when it was Mondays, we would go to Daddy's house on Sundays and now Monday. It would suck if I thought we were staying at your house for an extra day, but we actually weren't. I would probably get mad.

Mom: So, do you prefer to do things at the same time every day like dinner at five, snack at six twenty, or do you like it better without a schedule?

Cabbage: I like the schedule.

Anthony: I like things the same because I think it would be better because you can make plans.

Mom: So, when you run your own life in your own house, do you think you will have a rigid schedule and routine?

Anthony: Uh, yes and no. I think I would probably have more of a yes than a no because somedays my brain, I don't know…

Cabbage: I'd have a big YES.

Mom: Why?

Cabbage: Because I like being organized with everything.

Sometimes, we forget that our kids are people too, and there are times when we need to stop to think about what it's like to be in their little, smelly shoes. The world can be big and scary, and it looks bigger and more daunting the less information you have about what your day will bring and what expectations may be placed upon you.

What if you went to work not knowing that you would get into trouble that day because your boss wasn't consistent in what she wanted or expected of you? That situation would put even the most professional people on edge. Now, take that feeling and add it to an immature brain that is controlled by emotions. That's your kids without routines and schedules.

Routines and schedules can be a parent's best allies if they can master those skills. There are so many uses and benefits that it's worth implementing. These tools will ensure that things don't slip through the cracks, and the family will function together more seamlessly as a unit.

Chapter 4:

There Are No Good Cops or Bad Cops at the Parenting Police Force

M.O.M. SAID

Kids are like too-smart-for-their-own-good little monsters who are constantly testing the electric fence boundaries for weaknesses. All they need is one chance to sneak through the electrified fence of parenting rules, and you've got a B horror movie on your hands. Ooh, the carnage! Kids really will be kids, but one needs a strong enough parental constitution to be able to maintain a steady supply of power for that electrical fence so it doesn't fail. Get that backup generator gassed up; you're going to need it.

My kids ask over and over, "Why can't we stay up later?" "Because Mommy gets up at 4 am, and you need to go to bed before I do so that I can make sure you're not screwing around." "But we get to stay up later at Daddy's house." So clever of an argument in their little minds. "Do I look like Daddy?" I ask. "No." they chime together. "Have I ever let you stay up past 8:00 pm on a school night?" "No." "Well, what makes you think that I'm going to now?" Silence. I win.

No, this isn't the only thing my kids repeatedly try to get me to give in on, but the consistency I show them with enforcing routines and schedules gives me the power to keep my electric fence on.

I remember one incident when I was taking Cabbage to preschool, and he wanted a treat in the car. According to house rules, he hadn't earned one, but he wasn't going to give up, so for twenty minutes straight he cried and pleaded his case. By the time I pulled into the preschool, my nerves were shot, and my blood pressure was high, but I never gave in. Face red from angry tears, Cabbage took off into the corral of children. As I signed him in, I exclaimed in haggard victory, "I won! I won the battle!" and walked out with my head high, exhausted, and emotionally drained; a great way to start my workday.

Cabbage is my fighter. He has a fiery personality and a willpower to match my own, but I will fight him to the death to be the victor when it comes to my parenting rules. Anthony is my pacifist who abhors getting in trouble. Sure, he may roll his eyes or mutter under his breath, but he hardly ever puts up a real fight.

While having a strong will as a parent is great, it only works well if both parents are on the same page when it comes to setting, sticking to, and enforcing the rules. Parenting is hard enough without both parents having differing parenting styles. You know what I'm talking about: Good Cop vs Bad Cop. Traditionally, Dad played Bad Cop. "Just wait until your father gets home!" mothers would threaten. The Good Cop, Bad Cop method never works because the children know where the weak link is in the fence, they sneak through, and then the parents end up fighting over why one let their child do something that both parents agreed not to let them do.

If both parents are consistent in punishment, reward, boundaries, etc., there are no weak links in the fence for badly behaved little monsters to sneak through. In other words, both parents need to be in the same Parenting Police Force.

Being trained at the same Parenting Police Force Academy is great as a best practices theory, but how can you know what kind of parent your partner will be if you or he doesn't have kids? Can you just ask him and talk it out? Not necessarily. Theoretical parenting is NOT the same as actual parenting.

Most people go into parenting with the best intentions, wanting and hoping to stay strong in the harshest circumstances, but it's not that simple. If you are family planning with your significant other, you may want to agree with your partner on parenting guidelines, but when those little faces that look like yours are looking back at you and begging for what they want, some people cave in. I'm sorry, but if that's you, you're sucking, but it's not entirely your fault. Nature has tricked us into thinking that our children are the best-looking children on the planet so we won't abandon them. Fight that urge to give in.

I'm not a caver-inner. When my boys would give me the pouty face, I would say, "I made that face so I'm immune to its power. Sorry, I'm not changing my mind." People would always ask me how I could say no to those sweet, albeit very handsome faces, and I would tell them the same thing I tell my boys. I have a very strong intestinal fortitude when it comes to winning because I'm the parent, and, therefore, should be listened to and obeyed.

Okay, so if you can't determine from a conversation if your partner's and your parenting styles align, how can you know? I'm glad you asked. There are a few options here:

1. Try to get on the same page as much as possible, and then go for it. You'll have to learn on the fly and hope that both parties can stick to the same plan. If you find out you're not of the same strength of will, you will need to find ways to get onto the same page for the good of the family unit. It

WILL be hard, but nothing is unachievable with the right approach, love, and support.

2. **Use My PPP Method:** The Pet Parenting Preview Method (if the opportunity presents itself).

Have you heard people say that getting a dog is a good first step to having a child? If not, you just heard it. Regardless, the PPP Method offers you real-life scenario-based insight into how someone will be as a parent. If you or your partner have a pet, you can observe how your partner adheres to and enforces (or doesn't adhere to or enforce) agreed-upon boundaries with the pet in real time. Actions will always say more than words when you want to know the truth about how someone will be as a parent.

> *Dick and Jane have decided that it's time to discuss having children and expanding their family. In their many discussions about parenting, they feel they are on the same page regarding rules, boundaries, and punishment. However, Jane doubts whether they will both be strong enough to*

resist the manipulation of a little version of themselves.

One day, Jane's friend Sandy calls her in a frantic panic, "Jane, I have a family emergency, and I need to go out of town for a few months, but I have no one to watch my dog, Max! What am I going to do?!" "It's okay, Sandy. Dick and I can watch Max. Don't worry about him; you just go and take care of your family." Jane offers. "Thank you so much! You're a lifesaver, Jane! I'll bring him over tonight." Sandy says with a grateful sigh.

That night before Sandy comes over, Jane talks with Dick about how they can co-parent Max for the next few months. "I don't like it when dogs beg at the table for food. Do you think that we can agree that we shouldn't feed Max people food at the table?" Dick asks. "Sure. That makes sense," answers Jane. "Also," she notes, "We just got that new furniture in the living room. Let's try to keep him off the furniture, okay?" "Okay." Agrees Dick.

"What about sleeping in our bed? I loved it when I had a dog that slept by me at night," Dick offers.

"I would rather the dog sleeps in his bed at night since all that hair would be everywhere, and neither of us would likely get a good night's sleep," Jane suggests. "Okay, if that's what you think is best," resigns Dick.

A few hours later, Sandy shows up with Max, a beautiful golden retriever, and Jane and Dick are immediately in love. Who wouldn't love Max? He's a sweetheart of a dog, and he is just beautiful. "I can't thank you guys enough. Here's his food, his favorite toys, his bed, and his brush. Call me if you need anything." Sandy says as she kisses Max goodbye and rushes out to her car to race out of town.

Dick and Jane descend on Max with hugs and pats on the head. That first night, Max sleeps in his bed on the floor, and all goes well. In the morning, Jane receives a message from her boss that she needs to meet with an important client who is out of town, and she will need to pack an overnight bag and head to the meeting. "Sorry Dick," she says, "Do you think you'll be okay here with Max?" "Jane, I've had pets before. We will be fine," he assures his wife.

That evening, Dick orders a pizza and settles in on the couch with his beer and the remote. Smelling the meaty meat smell, Max trots over to the couch and rests his wet nose one inch away from the pizza box on Dick's lap. "You're not supposed to beg, and you're not supposed to have people food, but these are special circumstances. It's boys' night!" he rationalizes as he feeds Max a few pieces of pepperoni.

Drooling for more, Max coerces more pizza from Dick with those big doggy eyes and smiling face. Bedtime rolls around, but along with it comes a thunderstorm. Max starts whining and hides under the dining room table. "Now, what am I supposed to do?" Asks Dick to himself as he sighs. Tired and feeling bad for Max, Dick says, "Come on, Max, you can sleep with me just this one time." Up on the bed, Max jumps as he settles down peacefully to wait out the storm by Dick.

The next afternoon, when Jane arrives back at the house, she starts dinner and puts away her things. "How did last night go?" Jane asked Dick who was working from home to watch Max. "Great, honey. Just great." That evening as they sit down for dinner at the table, Max was resting his drooling mouth on Dick's leg. "What's this about?" asked Jane. "He didn't do that before. Did you give him food when you were eating?" she probed with suspicion. "Maybe," Dick replied sheepishly. "Dick, for real? I thought we were on the same page. As a dog dad, you suck, Dick!"

Tired from her trip, she dropped the argument. As she got into bed later that evening, Max immediately followed her. "Get off the bed, Max! Bad dog!" she yelled. Max looked confused as he hopped off the bed. "What's going on?" Dick asked as he slid into his side of the bed. Before Jane could answer, Max was back up on the bed, snuggled up next to Dick.

"Okay, what happened last night, Dick?" demanded Jane. "I leave for one day, and Max is a completely different dog. I thought that we agreed on the rules." "I know, but there was a thunderstorm, and he was scared, so I didn't think it would be a big deal if he slept in the bed one night," answered Dick.

Dick and Jane weren't on the same page as much as they both thought when it came to co-parenting. Dick was the softer parent (Good Cop), while Jane was more of a strict parent (Bad Cop). If they couldn't figure out a way to get on the same page, they were headed for parenting sucking and a potential rift in their marriage.

> *"Dick, we need to figure this out because we have Max for two months, and we need to get on the same page, or we will be fighting, and Max will be confused. Please put Max in his bed, and let's talk about this in the morning," said an exhausted Jane.*
>
> *Morning came, and the two talked over coffee about how important it is to co-parent Max with the same rules and consistency. "I get it, Jane", Dick agreed, "But I've always seen pets as family, and it's hard to say no." "Dick, your big heart is one of the things I love most about you, but I need you to try to stay consistent with Max for our marriage and for Max too," Jane cooed as she rubbed Dick's back. "I know. I'll try harder," promised Dick.*

Dick slipped up a few more times in the months to come, but eventually, he came around to see the logic in the consistent dog parenting terms they had agreed on. When it was time to say goodbye to Max, they were both sad, but they had learned some very valuable lessons about working together as a parenting team. Dog-sitting Max left them feeling more prepared to start their family.

No, pets aren't people, but if you think parenting a pet is hard and struggle to discipline or train your pet, you WILL struggle with parenting. The PPP Method is an easy way to get a preview or foreshadowing of someone's parenting style. I'm certainly not advocating for you to adopt a pet and return it after you've determined your partner's parenting style, but if your person has a pet, and it is not well-behaved and doesn't listen, then you know that your person will likely be more of a coddler and enabler (Good Cop) as a parent than a disciplinarian.

Be careful not to dismiss pet parenting as something completely detached from people parenting. I know we all believe what we want to believe, and we want to believe that our chosen partner will be a great parent because why wouldn't they? They love us, things will work out, and our children will be little angels. Um, how about no. Wanting to believe that you and your partner will be on the same parenting team because you love each other isn't a realistic outlook.

If the parenting team is divided and both parents are not the disciplinarian AND the fun parent, you will work against each other, and your children (and pets) will be worse off. Children are like animals: they can smell weakness. While their brains aren't fully developed until they are in their mid-to-late twenties, they learn very quickly which parent is the weak link and will play you against each other if you are not playing by the same set of rules.

Consistency across the board with your partner is key to your credibility as an authority figure. When you're a parent, parenting is usually not the only thing on your plate. The more exhausted or stressed you are, the more likely most people are to give into their child's irrational demands. "Oh, I'm at work so much that I don't want the time I spend with my kids to be all discipline, so I give in," I've heard people say. Just stop it, stop it right now.

I'm tired too, but it can be done. Unfortunately, there is NO break from parenting. You are never NOT a parent. Being a parent means it is your job to enforce structure, be consistent, and teach your children how to live within the rules and guidelines of society: your home's society first and then the world's society later. How will they ever learn to respect any kind of authority if you don't teach them to respect yours first?

When you are at your weakest, most tired point, turn to your parenting partner for help and support. You're on the same team. One of you should be able to enforce and hold the line when the other may not be as strong. If both of you are a combination of Good and Bad Cop, you can tag each other in with the knowledge that parenting will remain consistent. If you are a parenting team of one like I am when it's my turn for custody, you just need to keep reminding yourself that your sacrifice of energy, time, breath, and sanity will all be worth it and will make your life easier down the road. It will be worth it – I promise!

HER KIDS SAID

Mom: Okay, what time is bedtime at Mommy's house?

At the same time: Eight! (*Anthony*) Seven forty-five (*Cabbage*)

Anthony: 7:45 on a school day and just 8:00 or 8:15ish on a home day.

Mom: Okay, do you think that bedtime at Mommy's house makes sense even though it's earlier than you'd like.

Cabbage: Yes!

Mom: Why?

Cabbage: Because after a hard day, you should get more sleep.

Mom: (*Laughing*)

Anthony: Kind of, um, I don't know. I just think it should be a little bit later at least.

Mom: Even though you get up every morning at six for school?

Anthony: Yeah, because I feel like it's just a little early. (*Mumbling*) I have been complaining about the time...

Mom: Yes, I know. Why do you do as Mommy asks, even though you don't agree with or like it?

Anthony: Otherwise, you'll get in trouble, and you won't get any... something you would want like candy, or iPad, or YouTube or... (*Shrugs*)

Mom: Cabbage?

Cabbage: I should just do it because you're super nice, and you're beautiful.

Mom: Okay, that's a really weird reason. Uuuuummmm... When you know, there are rules about when we go to bed, when we leave for school, what is and isn't allowed for a treat if you don't finish your food, why do you sometimes fight against the rules?

Cabbage: Maybe because I was mad at school or something. I don't exactly remember.

Anthony: What do you mean, like after school?

Mom: No. Any rules that are always in place like the time for bed or the time for school. Why do you fight me on some of those things when they're always the same?

Anthony: Because I feel like it's too early or because we didn't get enough sleep...

Mom: So, because you didn't get enough sleep because you wanted to stay up later, you're crabby at me for the rules I set to get you enough sleep?

Anthony: No.

Mom: Do you see how that makes no sense?

Anthony: That makes sense... that makes sense.

Cabbage: Or because I got annoyed because before I got to school, I fell on my face...

Mom: So, in other words, you're taking out something that you were mad about in your life on me... okay. Let's think about that next time.

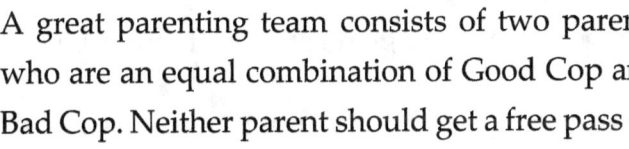

A great parenting team consists of two parents who are an equal combination of Good Cop and Bad Cop. Neither parent should get a free pass on doling out discipline or holding children accountable. While an imbalance of power may make one parent more liked by the kids, it will do the opposite with your spouse. A family unit only functions at its best when all authority figures are interchangeable in any circumstance regarding rules, consistency, and accountability. In units such as these, the partner bond becomes stronger where both parties feel as though they are putting in the same amount of effort in the good times and bad, and they are confident in their partner's parenting style when one needs to step away.

I cannot stress how important consistency is in parenting and how wonderful the results can be if you can tough it out. I have endured some zingers with my boys… days I remember crying while cutting up carrots in the kitchen after I battled with Cabbage for thirty minutes to go to bed. Or the time when I held onto Cabbage's bedroom doorknob from the outside as I heard him having an epic tantrum in his room, wondering what he was breaking and if I was doing the right thing and sticking to my rules.

Of course, I remember those times. The ones where you feel like the worst parent because your child is screaming at you that you're the worst parent. The times when you cry by yourself in your bedroom because you're so tired and emotionally drained from a battle you eventually won. The times when you talk to yourself like a crazy person and say, "What am I doing?!" I look back at those moments of strife, and I'm so thankful that I held my ground because I have two very well-behaved, polite little men.

Consistency is to parenting like muscle memory is to learning to ride a bike. The more you practice, the more your muscles learn what to do without thinking, and eventually, you can ride your bike (and ride it well) without any help. If you can be consistent in parenting, your children will learn good behavior patterns that they will eventually start to enact on their own simply because it has become ingrained in their way of life.

Chapter 5:

Fight for Your Right to Sleep

M.O.M. SAID

Ah, bedtime. Many parents have a love/hate relationship with bedtime. They love it because that means they get a "break" when their kids fall asleep, but they hate it because it can be the biggest battle of the day with their kids. Unfortunately, many adults already struggle with some sort of insomnia issue without adding in bedtime woes with little monsters. I don't think I know any other adults who say that they consistently get a good night's sleep, and it has nothing to do with their children: restless leg syndrome, anxiety or racing thoughts, a snoring partner, not enough time for sleep, you name it. Now take that crappy night's sleep and add in the complication of children who also do not want to sleep, and it gets ugly.

"Mommy, I'm scared", "Mommy, I don't want to sleep in my room", "Mommy, I had a nightmare", "Mommy, I'm an annoying little kid who is trying to find any excuse to say up", "Mommy, [insert annoying excuse of your choice here]." Tired parents are children's trap door into getting whatever they want in the moment they ask. Because of this weak gap in parental fortification, children end up sleeping in mom and dad's bed. Big mistake – HUGE!

If you give in even once to something you've said no to 1,000 times before, the only thing the child will remember is that one time you gave in, and they will refer to it over and over again.

Parent: "I said no."

Child: "But you let me do it that one time, remember?"

You've lost your parental footing because, in that moment of weakness, you sucked, and now you must pay the bedtime piper. The little monsters happily jump into the bed, and you prepare yourself for another sleepless night. Why? Beds aren't designed for 3, or 4, or 4.5, or however many adults, kids, and pets you're trying to Tetris into the bed.

Avoiding the co-sleeping arrangement is more difficult when your children are babies and toddlers. With my first baby, I tried to have him sleep in my bedroom in a pack-n-play, but his noises were annoying me, and he got kicked out and into his room in under two weeks. With my second baby, he went straight from the hospital right into the crib in his room. I mean, I may even have said to the nurses in the hospital the night I stayed there, "Take him to the nursery, and I'll see him in the morning." I had learned the value of sleep from the first go-round, and that first nursery night, I got a great night's sleep, putting me in the right headspace to bring home a new baby.

When my boys were tiny babies, I was deathly afraid to have "hold-me" babies... the ones that would cry when they weren't being held or would be poorly sleep-trained babies who would cry and expect a parent to appear immediately. No, that was NOT going to be me. I was going to parent on my terms. When my boys were old enough to sleep through the night and not need feedings during sleep time, I would make sure they were clean and fed, and then I would mute the baby monitor and go to sleep.

To some, that bedtime technique may sound a little extreme, but this methodology trained my children early on to self-soothe back to sleep, and I got enough sleep not to turn into a psychotic parent. Win, win. It takes a strong parent to ignore crying, but like I stated before, I have willpower that's as strong as a Spartan's courage in battle. When I muted the monitor, did they die? Let me check. Um, no.

> *Dick and Jane had finally been blessed with a little bundle of joy of their own, Joy. The first few years were hard but memorable, but when Joy turned two, it was time to transition her from crib to toddler bed. "I don't think it's going to be that big of a deal," said Dick as he lowered the crib bed and removed the front slats.*
>
> *The couple kissed Joy goodnight that first night and started walking out of her room. To their surprise, Joy was right on their heels. "Mommy!*

Daddy!" Joy cried as she held her arms up and jumped up and down, wanting to be picked up. "Joy, it's bedtime. You need to sleep in your own big girl bed now, okay?" Jane said in the sweetest tone she could muster after an exhaustingly long day.

"No Mommy! I want to be with you and Daddy!" she said as the first tear rolled down her sweet little flushed pink cheek. Dick looked at Jane, who was starting to cry tears of guilt, "Maybe you can sleep with us just this one time, Joy, okay?" reasoned Dick.

As all three tried to figure out their new sleeping positions, both Dick and Jane thought they had solved the problem. If they let Joy sleep in their bed, then they would get more sleep than if they had to keep getting up and putting her back into her room all night. They were wrong. The next evening, they tried again to talk Joy into sleeping in her bed. "You're a big girl now, Joy, and you get to sleep in a bed just like Mommy's and Daddy's," said Dick.

"Why can't I sleep in your bed again, Daddy?" asked Joy in her sweetest whine. "Because Mommy

and Daddy sleep in Mommy and Daddy's bed, and Joy gets to sleep in Joy's bed," he tried with his best convincing tone. As Joy started to cry again, Dick's exhaustion convinced him to give in and let Joy sleep in their bed again.

Night after night, week after week, month after month, Joy found a way to end up sleeping in her parents' bed. Sometimes, it started that way, and sometimes, she appeared at their bedside all creepy, like in those horror films where you wake up, and there's a pale child staring at you beside your bed.

Dick and Jane were letting their child make the parenting decisions, and they were sucking at setting boundaries, not co-sleeping, and getting any sort of decent sleep themselves.

So many of my good friends have let their children sleep in their beds, and not just once, it's every night! Not only is this practice not great for your quality of sleep, but it's also certainly not going to help your marital intimacy. Marital beds are for people in a marriage. Now, I'm not sure, but I suppose inviting your child into your bed could be a great excuse to get out of intimacy with your partner if you've overused the "I have a headache" line. If that is you, kindly refer to my first book, *Suck Less a Love: She Said, He Said Advice on Relationships*.

Dick was starting to get annoyed at the lack of quality sleep and lack of intimacy in his marriage since Joy had inserted herself into their bedroom at night. "Jane, we just can't keep letting her sleep in our bed. I can't function at work, and I miss sex," he bluntly argued. "Dick! Seriously. Joy gets so sad when she has to sleep in her room alone. Besides, how do you propose that we change the situation?" she asked.

"I don't know. I just know something needs to change." he sighed. "Well, I did read this article about letting your kids cry it out, but hearing her cry will break my heart, Dick," whined Jane. "Well, I'll try it tonight and see how it goes. You sleep, and I'll take the first night duty," he reasoned.

That first night was filled with a lot of in-and-out-of-bed trips, tears, and irrational words muttered out of sheer desperation. It yielded what seemed like no progress as Joy finally fell asleep on the floor of her bedroom, with Dick asleep not far away.

The next night was Jane's turn, and it broke her heart to see her little Joy so upset, but Dick and Jane had agreed that something needed to be done and that they were a team, so she fought the good fight. Joy stayed in her bed all night, and Jane fell asleep propped upright with her back to the doorframe right outside of Joy's room.

In the days and weeks that followed, bedtime became less of a battle, and eventually, Joy stopped asking to sleep in Dick and Jane's bed, and the whole family finally started to get some much-needed rest.

As my children transitioned from baby to toddler, I would watch them on the baby monitor, and as they sat up, I preemptively pushed the speaker button on the monitor and firmly warned, "Go back to sleep!" They would freeze, not knowing where the voice was coming from. It was hilarious to watch as if they were thinking, "God, is that you?" They would lie back down, and that was that.

Have my strict sleep rules paid off? You bet they have. My kids are great sleepers. I have never once let my children sleep in my bed, I have never slept in their rooms, and I do not allow them to come into my bedroom without knocking and waiting for a response. "Do not knock on my door unless you're sick or dying" is my mantra for bedtime. Mommy needs a good night's rest, or Mommy is scary, and no one wants that. My kids know how to avoid stepping on my sleep-deprived toes when I utter this line on my way to drop them off at school: "Mommy sleepy. Mommy need nap." They parrot my goofy phrase and giggle together from the back seat. They know that when Mommy is sleepy, Mommy gets a headache, and sleepy headache Mommy is not to be crossed.

A good night's rest is NOT highly overrated. For adults, sleep is such a gift. A sure sign that you know you're old is when you are excited to go to bed. If you're one of those people who understand the value of sleep because either you hardly ever get it and know how differently it makes you feel when you do, or you consistently get a good night's sleep and know how awful you'll feel without it, then you need to fight for your right to sleep.

HER KIDS SAID

Mom: What do you do in your room after iPad time but before you go to bed?

Leighton: Read.

Cabbage: Maybe read. (*Holding the cat on his lap in a position that is making her hate her life*) I used to make a book.

Mom: Make a book?

Cabbage: Yeah, make a book about Minecraft. There's a game called "Egg Wars" where I have to destroy the egg of the other team, and once kill them, like the other team, then they're out and you try to be the last team standing. And we are super good at that.

Mom: (*Confused about what the heck he's talking about.*) So, you made a book about it?

Cabbage: Yeah. Or I would just go straight to bed.

Mom: What time on school nights do you put yourself to bed?

Anthony: If I'm reading, then probably 8:30. But if I'm not, then it's 8:00 or 8:05 maybe.

Cabbage: Usually maybe 8:30 or just go straight to bed.

Mom: Do you want Mommy to get a good night's sleep?

Both: Yes!

Anthony: Otherwise, then you become crabby. Crabby head.

Mom: Under what circumstances do you think it would make sense to knock on my door at night or come into my bedroom?

Cabbage: Only when, um, you're really hurt or something like that. Or you're super sick.

Anthony: Or if like you're throwing up at night. Or if you… something's not going correctly.

Mom: Something that's not going correctly like what?

Anthony: Like probably you wake up and you immediately just like…

Cabbage: Collapse! (*As Anthony is standing and pretending to fall over*).

Mom: You wake up and collapse!? Has this happened before?

Anthony: When you wake up and you're dizzy as you're walking through the door.

Mom: So sick, in other words. Okay.

I know I'm old, and I love to sleep. Most days, I can't wait to crawl into bed, watch my five minutes of TikTok, and fall blissfully into what is usually a good night's sleep. I don't know how so many people can function without a consistent good night's sleep. My goofy husband, who hardly ever gets a good night's rest, said to me once, "I wish I could have another colonoscopy." "Why!?" I asked, shocked. "Because I got the best sleep when they knocked me out for it." he responded. What an absolute weirdo. But, I love him, and he's my weirdo.

That's how desperate people can become for something that is so unattainable but is so valued.

Sleep as a parent should NOT be something that you have to sacrifice. You already sacrificed your resources, your pre-kid body, your sanity, and your... well, pretty much everything. Sleep is something that you can get if you are a parent IF you are willing to fight the tough battle to get it.

Any sort of change with children will be difficult. It just will be. But sticking to your resolve with consistency will pay off with big rewards down the line. You will feel so much better and be in a much better headspace to be a good parent when you can get a good night's sleep. Nighty night, sleep tight and fight the good fight for sleep tonight. (I can come up with clever rhymes like this one because I get a good night's sleep!)

Chapter 6:

How to Behavior Train Your Child

M.O.M. SAID

Behavior training is either punishment-based or reward-based. One is an offensive strike, and the other is a defensive strike. You can either set a clear path to an earned reward, or reactively punish after something bad happens. Most parenting is a mix of the two because you can't anticipate every bad behavior and head it off with a reward system to prevent it. If there is a consistent problem that you've tried a few times to correct with punishment, then it's time to switch over to the reward system.

> *Little Joy isn't as little anymore. She's seven and in second grade, but all is not well in the world of Dick, Jane, and Joy. No, Jane is having regular meltdown fights with Joy every morning before*

school. For some reason, Joy is unwilling to get ready peacefully and on time, and both are starting their days off with tears and strife.

"I'm at my wit's end!" Jane confessed to her work bestie, Sandy. "Maybe you should try a reward system with Joy," her friend offered. "Like maybe come up with a good behavior chart that you can make together. Decide on what the reward will be after so many good mornings, and maybe that will help," suggested Sandy. "Ooh, well, Joy has been wanting to collect more of those little ponies. Maybe she could earn one each week. They don't cost much. Thanks for the idea, I'm going to try that!" said Jane.

On her way home from work, Jane stopped at the store to get a whiteboard and an erasable marker in Joy's favorite color. That evening, Joy and Jane sat down to make their reward chart, and Joy seemed excited at the opportunity to collect more ponies. As the week went on, there were a few little lapses in behavior, but as Jane reminded Joy of the reward they had discussed, Joy's behavior started to change. Soon, mornings became less of a battle and

> *more of a concerted team effort for positive behavior… and ponies.*

If you are working to correct bad behavior with the reward system, the goals need to be achievable, and the rewards need to be proportionate to the goal. In a scenario like Jane's, a whole week of good mornings could be rewarded with a $10 toy, a favorite treat, or stickers. A reward of a powered ride-on toy would NOT be a proportionate reward. As parents, it is our job to teach fair and equitable exchanges and to teach our children what realistic expectations and reciprocal rewards look like.

The key to implementing the reward system is again, consistency. You will get tired of how consistently I mention that consistency is important in all aspects of parenting, but it is the key to success. If you don't follow through on the promised reward, or if you change the terms of the agreement midstream, the system breaks, and you, as a parent, have failed. You're kind of sucking at behavior training.

Imagine if your boss gave you a clear roadmap to a promotion. "Do X, Y, and Z by this time, and you'll get a promotion," she explains. Great! Clear rules and metrics to achieve. You complete X, Y, and Z before the expected timeline, and excitedly and confidently, you walk into your boss' office to ask for your raise. "Sorry, I can't give you a raise based on X, Y, and Z. If you want it, you need to do A and B to earn that raise, and after you accomplish those things, we can revisit the raise," your boss explains.

Obviously, in this scenario, your boss is you, and you are your kids. I've been in this situation twice professionally, and it made me so angry for a long time. I lost all respect for my bosses and became extremely unmotivated at work because what was the point? The rules of engagement, promises, and trust were broken. What was my incentive to do a good job, be a model employee, or go above and beyond? There wasn't one. And that's when I started looking for a new job elsewhere. Those bosses needed to suck less... a lot less.

Your kids can't just adopt new parents if you have a parenting failure, so you need to realize the level of frustration and anger that they may feel if you aren't consistent in your reward-based behavior training. Children have fewer words to express feelings and less emotional control than we as adults, so they will act out those feelings in any number of bad behaviors, and the cycle of bad behavior and flawed behavior correction methods will continue. Correcting the methodology is on you, boss.

I haven't always gotten my behavior training ideas right the first time, but I've had some amazing successes. My favorite method for behavior training is the Skittles System. When it comes to incentive-based behavior training, I look for the largest return on investment for the least amount of actual investment on my part. The issue I was having day after day, week after week was motivating my children to put their devices down, get their shoes and coats on, and head out the door to leave for school in a timely fashion and without a great deal of griping. Fighting with your kids first thing in the morning puts a damper on everyone's day – Ask Jane! – so I invented the Skittles System.

"Boys, if you don't argue with me and get ready to go on time without any backtalk, I will give you each three Skittles in the car. If you sass me but still get ready on time, you get two Skittles, and if you make me late, you get none." A variation of this system applies for pickup from school. If you get in the car and start a fight with me about something, don't get off the playground in a timely fashion, or complain that I came too early for you to get to play enough on the playground, you get NO Skittles. If you are a good, compliant, pleasant child at pick-up, you get two Skittles.

There are more sub-guidelines to the Skittles System, like no asking Mommy for a "treat" until I'm on the main road because I'm trying not to hit children as I'm leaving the school grounds. If you ask for the Skittles while I'm on a side road or trying to get into traffic, you get fewer Skittles.

People laugh and shake their heads when I tell them about the Skittles rations, but it has been working for almost a decade. The only thing that has changed is the treat. I think it was candy corn for a while, but it didn't fare well in the car's heat and wasn't liked by both children equally. Skittles were their sweet spot, literally. For most people, a few Skittles wouldn't be enough to motivate anyone, but there are strict candy consumption rules in my house, so any extra is a huge deal.

A house rule also states that if you say you hate school, your teachers, or your homework, you get one of your favorite apps deleted from your iPad. Honestly, I hardly ever hear them complain about school after enforcing this rule for a year. It's awesome and is one of my favorite behavior-correction tricks.

The darker type of behavior training is discipline or the punishment-based method. Today, punishment means naughty chairs, time outs, or taking toys or electronic devices away. The key to success in this type of training is knowing what screws to turn to make your threats relevant. If you tell your child that if he does X again, there will be no treats after dinner, but he doesn't care for treats, you've set yourself up to fail. It's like if someone were to tell me that I couldn't wear jeans to work if I didn't do as they asked, the joke would be on them. I don't care for jeans and prefer skirts and heels.

Being the bad guy and being a disciplinarian is not synonymous. Being consistent and enforcing the rules is being a good parent. Sure, your kids will scream at you, hit you, throw things at you, and say hurtful or downright nasty things, but if you can maintain consistency with rules and consequences, it will yield amazing results.

There was a period of extreme frustration when my youngest seemed to want to fight with me about everything, and he seemed to value nothing. I used to tell people, "He just wants to watch the world burn." He was indifferent to everything I threatened to take away, and I was about to lose my mind. The only thing left that he placed any value on was his "baby", a tiny snuggle blanket with an elephant head in the middle. I didn't want to use baby as a hostage in negotiations, but nothing else was working. Unfortunately for me, following through on threats would mean that I would have to take baby hostage for the night, and that meant I'd have to deal with crying, melting down, and not going to bed.

It was a daunting lose-lose scenario for me. Concede the battle to the small monster (not an option) or be the person who stirs up the hornet's nest at my most tired time of the day. What did I do? I chose the harder path and suited up for battle. Why? Because I understood the importance of consistency, I knew it would all pay off at some point. It did. All those hours I spent in battle with him over the years, and now he's my sweet little minion, my personal assistant ready to do anything to help me. Sometimes, he even bows to me when he presents me with something I've sent him to the kitchen for. Last night, I asked him to get me a Sprite Zero, and he came back with it wrapped in a paper towel he taped on so it wouldn't be cold on my hands. Those things were his idea, not mine. We're a weird family.

Discipline and holding your children accountable also fall under the tough love umbrella. There's a reason it's called "tough" love because not only is it tough for the children, but it's even tougher for some parents to fight through the tantrums and manipulation that come from children when faced with tough love. Tough love requires a strength you must draw from deep within when you are in your most tired, stressed out, or emotionally drained state of being. What keeps me strong in these battles of wills with my children is the knowledge that I'm doing the right thing. I'm enforcing the rules and consistency just like the real world will do to your children, regardless of how you prepared them.

Our duty as parents is to train our children and prepare them for life in the real world. If we don't teach them how to live by the rules and that there are consequences, they will struggle with rules and authority when they become adults. Do you want that uncertainty and anguish for your children? No, of course, you don't. A child without tough love will struggle with tough bosses, teachers, rules of the road, and maybe even the law. Children who are taught to respect authority will function much better in a societal structure that relies on hierarchy and rules.

When parents don't have the steadfast resolution to hold their little monsters to the rules and guidelines set forth, that's what I call "soft parenting". In the heat of the moment, when it seems easier to give in than it is to take appropriate measures to stop the argument, crying, or drama, giving in will result in long-term harm to your child's psychological growth and maturity.

Let's say that a soft parent raises a child that always gets her way. What happens when she gets her first job from a boss who keeps trying to hold her work to a standard? She will rebel and quit or get fired. She won't understand or respect authority and will inevitably struggle as she constantly battles the system. When she finds herself repeatedly failing in the world, she will not understand why life isn't as easy as life was at home.

When I was in high school, I remember this girl who everyone thought was spoiled. She was given anything she wanted without having to work for it. On her sixteenth birthday, her parents gave her a brand-new car. What do you think that a teenager raised by soft parents did with that car? She ran it into their garage door the second week she had it. Why? Because she wasn't taught respect for authority. She also didn't understand responsibility because she was never held accountable for anything, and that was on the parents. They sucked big time.

I'm a huge advocate for tough love and strict parenting. "You're not strict, Mommy." my youngest Cabbage always tells me when he hears me ranting about being strict. "Being strict doesn't mean yelling, bud, it means that I hold you to a standard and don't let you get away with things," I explain. Effective discipline and behavior training need not involve raising your voice. There are other ways.

For instance, when both of my children are misbehaving together in what we parents refer to as sibling rivalries, my go-to form of punishment-based behavior training is The Shirt. To the layperson, the threat of a piece of clothing seems meaningless, but in my house, The Shirt strikes fear into the hearts of small, bickering monsters.

Years back, I bought a patterned polyester blend short-sleeved shirt for my husband at a fashion-forward store, and I thought it would look great on him. It did, but he told me that he would never wear it because he said it made him look ambiguous. One day, when my children would NOT stop fighting, I haphazardly cut the neck hole larger, and I told them to get into the shirt together. They squeezed in, and as they were nose-to-nose, they scowled at each other and tried to get as far away as the stretch in the shirt would allow.

I played the song "Friends" by Michael W. Smith on my Alexa speaker, and I told them that they had to remain in the shirt for the duration of the song, and if they didn't, they would be put back into the shirt, and the song would start all over again until they made it through one whole song. The process is always the same: they start out bickering, then they give in to the punishment, and by the end, they're goofing off and laughing together. Before I release them from The Shirt, I make them recite "The Brother Creed" which I make up every time.

Repeat after me: "I'm sorry for fighting with you, and I promise to try harder to be nice. You are the only brother I will ever have, and I love you." Then, I make sure they apologize to me for their fighting, and then they run off together, bonded in a union against The Shirt. It's like how the enemy of my enemy is my friend. The enemy of their enemy is The Shirt, and so they end up friends. Not only is this method effective, but it's also hilarious to watch. Give it a try, and help your children suck less at arguing.

HER KIDS SAID

Mom: What are the rules for "treat" on the way to school?

Cabbage: So, when Mommy calls you down like, "It's time for school!" if you don't do it right away then you won't get that much skittles, but if you do it right away, you get three, maybe four Skittles.

Mom: Under what circumstances do you get none or two?

Anthony: If you don't hurry up.

Cabbage: If you argue or if you don't even do it or ignore...

Anthony: ... And then you are late so...

Mom: What are your favorite Skittles to get?

Cabbage: Red or blue.

Anthony: Uh, red or orange.

Mom: If you knew there was no reward for getting in the car on time in the morning, would you still get ready as quickly and compliantly?

Cabbage: No.

Anthony: No, not as fast.

Mom: Anthony, if you know you're not going to want the treat in the car before school, why do you still get ready to go on time and without complaining?

Anthony: So I don't lose something that I want or really don't need but I wanna have later in the day.

Mom: So, it's nothing to do with the Skittles then, you're thinking ahead for the other things you don't want to lose?

Anthony: Yeah

Mom: What is worse, losing Minecraft, losing YouTube Kids, or not getting some regular, supervised YouTube time at the end of the day?

Anthony: Minecraft!

Mom: Minecraft is the worst to lose?

Anthony: Well, let's see. (*Pauses*) Yeah because then you have to get all of that stuff back.

Mom: Cabbage? (*As he's melting into the couch with boredom*)

Cabbage: YouTube Kids.

Mom: How do you feel – sit up. This is an important question. How do you feel about "The Shirt" when you guys are fighting?

Anthony: The Shirt… it's kind of crammy, and it's like weird. It just doesn't feel good because we're just like this (*Leans over and hugs his brother tightly as Cabbage fakes choking*). It feels odd, you know what I mean?

Cabbage: It feels like (*makes slurping, squishing noises*).

Mom: So, do you like having to have The Shirt?

Cabbage: No.

Anthony: Sometimes it's by myself so yes.

Mom: No, it's never by yourself. It's for when you two are fighting (*rolling my eyes*). What do you think is the worst punishment at my house?

Anthony: Uummmmm... Losing...

Cabbage: iPad for ten days...

Anthony: (*Laughs*) It would never be ten days.

Mom: That's what happened when you broke your iPad.

Cabbage: Yeah, that's what I mean.

Mom: That's a good answer. What about you, Anthony?

Anthony: I don't really have an answer to this one, but it's probably kind of what Dude said but a little bit different.

Mom: Losing your iPad? Cabbage, sit up.

Anthony: Yeah, or having no treat for quite a while.

Mom: (*Cabbage now lying on the ground in front of the couch*). Sit up. We are going to take a break after this last question. What do you think the worst punishment is for a child anywhere?

Cabbage: Uhhhh…

Anthony: Probably not having any fun, probably having no devices or anything, no food…

Mom: No food?!

Anthony: Yeah, no nothing. That's the worst punishment ever, right?

Cabbage: Oh, I know, I know! No fun, no devices, um, ahhh…. Being grounded.

Mom: Do you even know what that means?

Cabbage: Yeah, you get stuck in your room, and people have to bring food or water up to you.

Mom: It's not jail!

Cabbage: Or when you break a window.

Mom: Yeah, you did break a window. But that's not punishment.

Anthony: I haven't broken anything for a while.

Cabbage: Yeah right!

Anthony: I broke that picture upstairs.

Mom: Yeah, I know. I was just going to bring that up.

Cabbage: What picture?

Anthony: The one that used to hang by my door.

Mom: Yes, when you slammed your door really hard and it fell and broke.

Anthony: Yeah, but did I slam it really hard?

Mom: Yes, because you were throwing a tantrum.

Cabbage: What door?

Mom: His bedroom door.

Cabbage: Yeah, but there's no glass there.

Mom: This was years ago, but now it's not there because it broke.

Anthony: But that's pretty much the only thing that I did.

Behavior training is hard no matter what ages your children are. Either they are really young and are overly run by their emotions, or they are older and are run by their hormone-fueled attitudes. The good news is that behavior training can be successful if you can do the following:

1. Determine what they value most and be ready to leverage it if needed.

2. Make up a system where you can make as little investment as possible to get the largest ROI from your children.

3. Be consistent in your rewards or punishments and the rules surrounding them.

If you don't figure out a way to behavior-train your child, it will make their ability to function in other settings very difficult: school, birthday parties, sleepovers, jobs, life, the world, etc. Not having a realistic knowledge of how the world works and how harsh it can be is something your child will end up having to learn the hard way if you don't find a way to train them at home.

Parents don't want their children to struggle as they are put into new situations that life will inevitably present to them. The best way to help your children is by taking the bullet, so to speak, for them and managing life's hard adjustments with their futures in mind. Good behavior training will benefit you and them exponentially as a family unit and as they find their way in the world.

Chapter 7:

Play Dates Aren't Just for Kids

M.O.M. SAID

When Dick and Jane had Joy, they asked Dick's mom if she would babysit Joy while they went to work. While the solution was alluring from a cost and convenience standpoint, Dick and Jane were starting to notice that Joy was becoming a very shy child.

One Saturday morning, when Jane took Joy to the grocery store with her, Jane ran into her friend Sandy. "Oh hi, Jane! Who is this little dolly you have with you?" Sandy squealed as she crouched down to kid level. Jane looked around for Joy and the tiny cart she was pushing, and she didn't see her. The light tugging on her pant leg made her realize that Joy was hiding behind her. "Joy, come meet my friend, Sandy," she urged.

No movement. Joy held on tighter to Jane's leg, and Jane decided it was best to leave her in her social bubble. "Sorry, I guess she's a little shy," confessed Jane. Usually running her errands without Joy, Jane didn't realize how introverted Joy was becoming from lack of socialization, and she started to worry.

When I decided to have children, I silently vowed that my kids would not be little hide-behind-mommy kids. Was that even a genetic possibility with my extroverted personality and that of their father? Like two negatives equaling a positive, could two extroverts equal an introvert?

My first husband and I agreed that during the first few years of their lives, we would have our children cared for at home to avoid the onslaught of diseases that they would happily share with us from other kids at a childcare facility. Neither of us wanted to get sick every other week, and we both worked from home, so in-home childcare made the most sense.

The younger your children, the harder it is to avoid their getting sick, and the harder it is to treat them for illness. The downside to our in-house childcare plan of isolating our children was that we were setting our kids up to suck at socialization. What was our answer to helping our children be well-adjusted, social, and personable? The play date.

Let's be real: kids need socialization just like pets, and both will bite if not trained properly. At baptism classes at our church, we made friends with a couple who had a baby the same age as our first, and the play date was born. The great thing about play dates when you have babies is that you just use the play date as an excuse to get together with friends, gripe about parenting, and drink as your babies sleep next to each other in their carriers.

However, as our babies got older and both families grew to families of four, the play dates got less relaxing. The children had someone to play with other than the parents, and we still got to hang out with our friends, but the constant running off to prevent accidents was added. It was almost like a mini version of a gladiator blood sport as we watched our clumsy toddlers fight over toys, fall, and cry as we watched from the cheap seats.

Dick and Jane got invited to a family barbecue at Dick's office. The smell of ashy charcoal ablaze mingled with the laughter of small children as they chased each other around in the grass. Parents clustered in small groups, talking about work while overindulging in chips, brats, and potato salad.

Amidst the excitement, Jane sighed as Joy clung to the hem of her mother's skirt. Bending down, Jane said to Joy, "Honey, why don't you go play with those kids over there? They have those little ponies that you like. Let's go over and see if they have ones that you don't, okay?"

Nodding in silence, Joy slowly walked over to the small cluster of girls and their prize ponies. "Hi, girls. This is Joy. She likes ponies too. Do yours have names?" Jane started. "Oh yes, of course!" One confident little girl exclaimed. "This one is Princess Pickle Tail because she's pink but has a green tail," she continued.

"I have that one too," Joy whispered to Jane's astonishment. "Really? What's yours named?" The little girl asked. "Princess Ivy," Joy answered. "Oh cool! We both named our ponies 'Princess'. Why Ivy?" The girl persisted. "Because my mom has an ivy plant that's green." Joy elaborated as she kneeled next to the new girl. "I like you. My name is Poppy," announced the chipper little girl as she held out her little hand to Joy.

Joy looked at Jane with a confused look. "Shake her hand, Joy. Maybe you and Poppy can play ponies while I go get some lunch with Daddy. Is that okay?" she asked Joy. "Sure, Mommy," said Joy without even looking at her. And that was it. Poppy had passed one of the pre-interview screenings to be put on the play date shortlist.

By the time my youngest reached the toddler stage, we had a play date circuit: three families with which I scheduled regular play dates. As my kids got older and I became a play date expert, I added other guidelines for play dates, and patterns started to emerge:

1. If you were a new family, you got the morning play date slot of 9:00 am – 11:00 am. This time slot was for vetting compatibility in parenting styles, vetting if my kids would get along well with your kids, and there was no commitment of food or a meal of any sort. Sharing food was reserved for veteran play date families.

2. If you were invited to a dinner play date, you were in. Whoever was hosting made dinner, and the guest family brought dessert. Hosting the event went back and forth between families every other time. Dinner play dates started at 4:00 pm and ended around 6:30 or 7:00 pm, depending on bedtimes. The dinner play dates were allotted more time for BS-ing without the get-out-of-my-house-before-lunch time crunch.

3. If your parenting style wasn't a match for mine, or if your children didn't play well with mine, you became a dinner or lunch friend – no kids.

4. I started to realize that every other play date would end up being canceled because someone's kid was sick.

5. You will learn what toys to get your kids because someone else has that toy, and your child loves it.

6. If you want to have more play dates, you need to make sure to schedule the next play date at the end of the current play date, or it just won't happen. (Or don't schedule it then if you want to use the excuse, "I'll be in touch.")

For a certain time of your children's lives, play dates can serve many purposes for them and you. Even if your child attends a daycare, you and they can both benefit from play date socialization. Your children will learn to communicate effectively with other children and adults, and you will get some much-needed adult commiseration time that you can't otherwise get without a babysitter.

When your children reach late elementary school age, play dates can have a drop-off-and-forget kind of bonus. The caveat there is that if you drop your child off at someone else's house for a play date, you better be ready to reciprocate that favor, so be sure you like that child enough to invite them into your home for extended periods.

HER KIDS SAID

Mom: Do you remember play dates that we've hosted?

Cabbage: (*Distracted by the cat who has finally escaped his grasp and is running away*) What?

Mom: Do you remember the play dates that we have hosted?

Anthony: No.

Cabbage: What does "hosted" mean?

Mom: Had at our house. When everyone used to participate in the play date.

Both: (*Confused silence*)

Mom: A play date is a family that comes here that comes for an arranged period of time.

Anthony: Oh yeah, her? The kids, the kids (*as he points to the back door*).

Mom: Why do you think that parents plan play dates for their kids?

Anthony: For fun.

Mom: For fun for whom?

Cabbage: For the kids! (*Raising both hands in victoriously answering a question right*) Because they earned it.

Mom: (*Yelling to husband in the kitchen, who is making a racquet*) Could you make MORE noise?

Anthony: Because the kids are bored and don't do anything active, and you have the time to do it, so why not have... (*Inaudible because my husband is still making too much noise in the kitchen*).

Mom: (*Turning to husband in the kitchen*) Oh my gosh! Are you done?! (*Turns back to the kids*) What would your ideal play date look like?

(*More loud noises from the kitchen*)

Mom: WOULD YOU PLEASE STOP THAT!

(*Husband laughs from the kitchen as he does the dishes*)

Mom: What would your ideal play date look like? Like if I said, "We are having a play date."

In your little child brain, what would be super fun for you on a play date?

Cabbage: (*Yells the name of a friend*)

Mom: Just one person? That's it?!

Anthony: (*Laughing and checking out of the conversation as he folds himself over a pillow and buries his head in the couch*).

Mom: No activity?

Cabbage: Yeah, we'd do Harry Potter like last time.

Mom: Okay. Anthony? Anthony, sit up.

Anthony: Probably one, two, three, five friends. Possibly four friends.

Mom: Doing what?

Anthony: Like five friends doing a lot outside if it's not cold. Like play tag, or see who can last the longest with guns and stuff… and probably some video games too.

Cabbage: (*Raising hand and bouncing up and down*) OOH! Do like maybe (*names 5 friends*)…

Mom: Doing what?

Cabbage: Um, playing on the Wii, maybe playing ultimate hide and seek.

Mom: What's the difference between regular hide-and-seek and ultimate hide-and-seek?

Cabbage: Um, there's gonna be, uh, one hider and five taggers.

Mom: So, it's about the amount of people playing that makes it "ultimate"?

Cabbage: Yeah. And I'm also gonna play battle arena. (*Starts making gun noises at his brother*)

Play dates are like real dates. The first dates are casual and are easily escapable because you are still vetting for long-term viability. Dating in both instances becomes more serious as dinner and drinks become involved.

While finding friends you like and who have the same parenting style as you do is not an easy task, it's well worth trying to find those friends. If your kids are roughly the same age, that's even better. Plus, kids love to play with other kids' toys. They even love to play with the same toys in a new setting like how cats become interested again in an old cat tower once the tower has moved to a different location. What's old becomes new, and you can use that fact to your advantage.

Other fringe benefits to finding play date besties are new recipes, new couple friends, and an expanded social network. While your children may or may not remember all the effort you made to find and plan those play dates, they will certainly emerge on the other end with greater skills in negotiation, sharing, and manners.

Chapter 8:

Think Outside the Tooth Fairy Box

M.O.M. SAID

The Tooth Fairy is real in my house; you'd better believe it. Even if you don't, my kids do, and that's what's important. I remember the Tooth Fairy leaving me a quarter under my pillow and being super excited. How did my parents pull that off? They had way more patience than I ever will. How would I pull off the Tooth Fairy bait-and-switch with my limited patience and lack of sneaky spy moves?

Dick and Jane realized that they needed to think fast one afternoon when Joy lost a tooth. "Dick! What did your parents do when you lost a tooth?" Jane asked frantically as she checked her watch to see how much time they had to get on the same page with a plan. "Um, I think that we just left the tooth under our pillow and got a dollar?" Dick explained, unsure of what his memory was telling him.

"Is that what we want to do with Joy? My parents had me put the tooth in a special felt envelope on which my mom embroidered 'My Tooth'. I don't have time to do something like that," shrieked Jane, panicking about the time and creativity she was lacking at the moment.

"Jane, calm down. It's just the Tooth Fairy." Dick tried to help but only ended up making matters worse. "Dick! This is Joy's childhood memories that are at stake here!" she argued. "Okay, why don't I pick up a roll of pennies from the bank since I have to stop there anyway? Maybe you can put the tooth in that little box you got on our honeymoon, and we can create our own Tooth Fairy, okay?"

"I love you, Dick! I think that's a great plan. I'll see you at dinner in a few hours," sang Jane, happy to have married a man who loved her enough to diffuse her calmly when she was in full freak-out mode.

Just like Dick and Jane, I got creative and concocted a unique version of the Tooth Fairy. There are no rules for how a parent fakes certain mythical beings' existence. I customized the Tooth Fairy to suit my parenting style, and here's how I did it:

Problem: How to make the exchange without having to enter the children's rooms. I was not about to sneak in and try to put something under their pillows. That's lunacy. Ain't nobody got time for that, especially tired moms with terrible hand-eye coordination after six pm.

Solution: Make a custom Tooth Fairy box that would be placed outside of my children's bedrooms. The box is much too large to fit under a pillow, and the Tooth Fairy likes to run an efficient trip, so she prefers to access the box outside the room.

- **Step 1.** Go to the craft store and purchase a large, unfinished wooden box with a hinge and closure.

- **Step 2.** Decorate the box with tooth images and the child's name. Paint the outside gold or silver and black on the inside to replicate a treasure chest.

Problem: How to get children to go to bed on time the night of the Tooth Fairy's arrival.

Solution: Tell them that the Tooth Fairy is a very busy lady and she has them penciled in for (insert children's bedtime here). If they're not asleep when she arrives, she will move on without making the exchange because she's busy and on a schedule. (She sounds like a lady Mommy would get along well with. Maybe she and I should plan a play date.)

Problem: How to make the Tooth Fairy convincingly real.

Solution: Dream up a backstory and hype it up. Our Tooth Fairy is an iridescent, colorful hummingbird-like being who is based on the imagery of the one from an animated movie about popular mythical beings. She leaves calling cards that have her photo on them, along with the child's name and the date. She also leaves multi-colored feathers scattered in and around the tooth box because she's stressed out and is molting.

Problem: How to be prepared for when a tooth falls out randomly, like at dinner time in a Laffy Taffy, which has happened at my house.

Solution: Have little trinket toys on hand and hidden, and always have cash and pre-printed calling cards ready to go. One of my kids lost two teeth in two days. Sadly, I was not prepared for the second tooth, and I sent out the husband on a late-night run for a toy.

While my Tooth Fairy ideas have served me well, there have been a few complications. "Mommy, how come the Tooth Fairy leaves us $5 at your house and $20 at dad's house?" Crap. Think fast, think fast! "Because the Tooth Fairy leaves toys here at my house. The box is bigger here, so she makes exceptions to her normal rules." Sounds convincing, doesn't it? I'd believe me, so they did too.

It's so cute to see them in the dark hallway of the morning, going through their boxes and talking to each other about what had transpired overnight. One of my boys even asked for a special container to keep his Tooth Fairy calling cards in. Adorable.

Santa in my house has a special personality too. I have tailored my Santa to suit my parenting and lifestyle just as you, as a parent, have the right to do. Here's how Santa has adapted to my house rules:

Problem: How to make Santa's gift-giving fair and equitable.

Solution: Santa only leaves one present for each child and fills the stockings. All the other gifts are from the actual people who purchased the gifts. I think that Mommy should get the credit for spending all that money on those gifts, not Santa! Furthermore, the kids need to be nice to Mommy leading up to Christmas because Mommy has the power to return items she's purchased just as easily as Santa can put a child on the naughty list.

Santa also only gives one gift to preempt the issue of my kids telling other kids that Santa got them something better than Santa gave the other children. As a parent, I don't think it's fair to make your Santa play favorites amongst households because of the resources of the parents. My Santa gives low- to mid-level items like board games, and he fills the stockings with inexpensive trinkets and candy.

Problem: How to explain how all the wrapped gifts match my color-coding system, even the ones from Santa.

Solution: Christmastime at my house means that everyone's gifts are wrapped in a different pattern of gift-wrapping paper. I started this tradition so it would be easier on Christmas morning to tell whose gifts were whose without the annoyance of tags or reading for kids who couldn't read yet, making the whole ordeal inefficient.

I waited for the day when my children would ask me, "Mommy, why are the gifts from Santa wrapped in your wrapping paper?" I had such a good comeback for that question, but it still hasn't been asked! "Well, Santa has known Mommy for a very long time, and he knows how neurotic I am about having things done my way to match. When he comes here with your gifts, he uses my wrapping paper; that's his gift to me. The gift of visual continuity." Maybe I'll get to use that line... just maybe.

Problem: How to eat the milk and cookies when you're trying not to gain holiday weight.

Solution: Only have the kids put out enough cookies that you are comfortable consuming. You can't throw them away because that leaves evidence. Unless, of course, you are prepared to sacrifice your cookies to the garbage disposal.

Problem: How to make Santa's visit believable.

Solution: Have someone with different handwriting write out a Thank You note from Santa and leave it by the empty cup and plate. Yes, I've done this Santa hack, and my youngest has those Post-its on the wall of his bedroom right next to the Post-it I that I stuck on a dollar bill as payment for cleaning toilets! "For cleaning toilets" is right next to "Thank you for the milk and cookies, Santa." Yeah, we're a weird family.

HER KIDS SAID

Mom: What is your favorite thing about the tooth fairy?

Both: Money!

Anthony: And you get just random toys.

Cabbage: And fun toys!

Mom: What does she look like?

Cabbage: A pixie!

Anthony: She has colorful wings (*stands up and gestures wings*), like down this way, and she's kinda small.

Mom: She's tiny?

Anthony: She's not that tiny, but not that big too.

Mom: So, she's like six inches tall?

Anthony: (*Shows a space of about a foot between his hands*) She's like this tall.

Cabbage: She's like this tall (*shows a space of about four inches between his fingers*).

Mom: So, yours is a foot tall, and yours is four inches tall?

Cabbage: Well, because how are they supposed to get through your door?

Anthony: They don't.

Mom: They're magic people... okay?

Anthony: They fly through the window!

Mom: What do you think about the things she leaves you?

Cabbage: (*Mostly on his back with his foot in the air*) Nice.

Anthony: Nice because she might have bought her own stuff or made her own stuff.

Mom: So, you think that she's nice because of the amount of effort she puts into it or the money she puts into buying it?

Both: Yeah.

Anthony: Probably a lot of like...

Cabbage: (*Interrupting*) Wait! I just realized, when they leave money and the tooth is gone, they pretty much bought your tooth.

Mom: Yeah, that's kind of weird, isn't it?

Cabbage: It's kind of cursed.

Anthony: And then they talk to people's teeth.

Mom: Why do you think she likes to visit our house?

Anthony: Because we are nice and… yeah.

Cabbage: Because… Like Anthony said.

Anthony: And because we earned it with our teeth coming out. And it's only once in a while.

Mom: Have you ever seen or heard her?

Both: No.

Anthony: Because if you've seen her, she would have been gone by the time you woke up… it's impossible, I pretty much think. But you can hear her if you're really lucky.

Cabbage: Trap her!

Anthony: You can't trap the tooth fairy. It will fly through the window or something like that. But anyways, you can probably hear her.

Mom: What would she sound like?

Anthony: Probably like little wings (*gesturing with finger movements of little wings and making sssss sounds*), and probably like talking quietly.

Mom: She talks to herself?!

Cabbage: What the?!

Anthony: She probably talks to the people… how do her wings slash feathers come off?

Mom: She's stressed out. I've told you this.

Cabbage: (*Sitting up now from a slumped position*). Wait, what?

Mom: You know, when birds get stressed out, they molt which means they lose feathers, like when you stress out as a person, you lose hair. She's stressed out – she has a lot to do… she loses feathers.

Cabbage: That was a TON of feathers!

Mom: Yeah, well, she's got a big job! Okay, why do you think Santa fills only the stockings and gives one gift to each of you?

Cabbage: (*Raising his hand while I'm still asking the question*) OOH! I know this one! Because, um, he has like, every kid in the whole wide world.

Mom: That's right.

Anthony: And cuz it's a ton of money, and if you did multiple per person, that would probably take more than the entire night. Because it would be like the next day, and you would still be throwin' stuff, and he has to do it in a certain amount of time.

Mom: What do you think about the gifts that Santa brings? Are they any good?

Cabbage: Yes! Definitely.

Anthony: Yes, and no. More yes than no.

Cabbage: Next year, I want to get something good.

Mom: Anthony, what did you say?

Anthony: I said, "More yes than no". Sometimes I don't like it.

Cabbage: Then you can give it to me!

Mom: Sit up. I can't see your faces. Have you ever seen or heard Santa?

Cabbage: Yes!

Anthony: No. You have NOT heard Santa.

Cabbage: Yes, I have.

Anthony: (*Making an annoyed face*). Oh, come on.

Cabbage: Maybe at like one, two, or twelve at night, and I heard something on the roof, and I didn't know what it was.

Mom: So, what did you do when you heard it?

Cabbage: Just went back to sleep because I was worried that um, if he knew that I was awake, I would just get coal.

Mom: Yeah, that's right. Or cat poop.

Cabbage: EEW!

Leighton: Yeah, but there's no chimney in the house, so where…

Mom: Haven't I shown you that movie and how that works? How do you think that he can eat all the cookies every child leaves out?

Cabbage: He's magical.

Anthony: He has a big diet.

Mom: He diets all year for the one day he eats only cookies?

Anthony: No, he eats like nothing before then.

Cabbage: That's a good question.

There are infinite possibilities for you to reinvent your mythical creatures, make special memories for your children, and keep your sanity. Just because someone else did it one way in the past does NOT mean that you must do it that way too. Why torture yourself trying to wait until kids are so sound asleep that they wouldn't hear the creak of their doors opening or feel the movement of your late-night-ungraceful hand feeling around underneath their pillow?

Who even came up with that idea in the first place? The parent of a narcoleptic? Like I said before, no parent has the time for that stupidity. If you do and you have, good for you. You suck less than I do at the bait and switch and likely have a greater degree of patience than I do. When it comes to mythical creatures, I prefer to make my own as I tend to make my own rules for a lot of things in my life.

I cannot wait for the day when my kids get older and tell me how much they enjoyed the little rituals around Santa and the Tooth Fairy. However, sometimes families engrain things so deeply in a child's mind that they start to think it's normal… like how my parents put pickles in the chili and served it with rice. Took me a long time to figure out that only my family did that. Regardless of how weird your family's rituals are, they will make wonderful lasting memories and great stories to share when they get older (hopefully with their families and friends, not with their therapist).

Chapter 9:

It's a Tradition to Have Traditions

M.O.M. SAID

The Tooth Fairy and Santa are just part of the opportunities you have to make wonderful traditions for your family. When people look forward to having a family, one of the things they imagine in an idealized thought bubble is the traditions that they'll make and keep with their little cherubs. I can still vividly remember our family's traditions from when I was little, as odd as they may seem to anyone outside the family.

Christmas Day was like Christmas times three. The morning started at our house, lunch was at Grandma and Grandpa's house across the street (where my dad always fell asleep on the floor after, and my mom got annoyed with him because we still had one more Christmas to attend). Then it was into the car for an hour and a half drive to my other Grandparents' Christmas gathering with a million relatives, and then I would fall asleep on the drive home. I loved it – so many Christmases in one day, but as a parent, I realize that the plan was legit insane.

We had other weird traditions for Christmas, like coming down the stairs on Christmas morning and ringing a little golden apple-shaped bell to alert the parents that we were ready and anxiously waiting for Christmas to start. I wonder what happened to that bell…? I can still hear Christmas music and smell the egg bake as I recall my sister and I sitting impatiently giddy at the bend of the staircase. When the stage was set perfectly for a magical sight, we were called to come down the stairs to the wonder that was Christmas morning. First, we opened stockings, then we were tortured by being made to take a break to eat the Christmas morning egg bake, then presents followed, and then on to the two other Christmases mentioned above.

When we went across the street to Grandma's and Grandpa's house, we knew that we were going to get the once-a-year Christmas dessert: suet pudding, aka spotted dick, aka figgy pudding, aka it's weird unless you grew up with it. I LOVE suet pudding. Yes, it sounds gross, looks weird, and is filled with fat (that's what suet is), but I must have it at Christmastime, or it's not Christmas! My Grandma made two sugar and butter-based warm sauces to go on top: lemon and vanilla, and each had its respective ceramic pour pot. The lemon one had a smaller, round, pink-tinted pot, and the vanilla had a long, white gravy boat. One of the best things about the suet pudding tradition is watching new family inductees, or children, as they get old enough to eat it, suffer through their first bites. Why? It's an acquired taste.

When I started my own family, I was so excited to start my own traditions. I adopted the stockings first, followed by the tortuous break to eat breakfast. I tried the egg bake breakfast tradition, but no one liked it, so I tried to do a Christmas dinner of red Belgian waffles with green homemade peppermint whipping cream topped with holiday sprinkles. That food tradition lasted a few years before I retired it due to a lack of participation and enthusiasm. Christmas dinner has now become more practical: lasagna made the day before, and gingerbread bars made the day of. Anthony helps me make the lasagna, and Cabbage helps make the dessert. After all, the house still needs to smell like holiday food on the actual holiday.

A week or two before Christmas, we always bake and decorate cutout cookies. I decided years ago that cut-out cookies from scratch were my favorite cookies of all time, and I got the best recipe for those cookies and homemade frosting from my first play date mom friend!

As my children got older and wanted to help more in the kitchen, cookie decorating became a family affair. Cutouts are a multi-day process: three to be exact.

Day 1 is for making the dough and letting it chill for at least 24 hours.

Day 2 is for rolling, cutting, and baking.

Day 3 is the day Mom makes all the royal icing from scratch with different tips and sets up all the workstations. Everyone gets an apron, and the decorating commences. The kids usually lose interest about 8-10 cookies in, leaving mountains of cookies left to be hand-decorated by the adults.

Taking a step backward on the holiday calendar is Halloween, Cabbage's second favorite holiday. He loves everything spooky or blood-and-guts related. Halloween is our other cookie-decorating tradition, but this one is more break-and-bake than made from scratch. I buy all the holiday-themed edible shapes: zombie hands, eyeballs, knives and axes, tombstones... all the cool toppings that cost a small fortune and will crack a tooth when you eat them but will look amazing when placed in blood-red icing.

The Easter traditions became cumbersome because of my oversight. When the kids were first born, I made the stupid mistake of ordering customized Easter baskets online without looking at the dimensions of the baskets. My bad. They are enormous, so every year, I have problems trying to fill them. Filling the cavity is like buying gifts for another Christmas. However, I've figured out a workaround of sorts. I buy the three-foot-tall chocolate rabbits from the warehouse store, and that fills most of the basket up. The tradition now is pretty much just the anticipation of the rabbits that come to a horrific fate when I chop them up into tiny pieces for after-dinner treat negotiations.

> *In the first few years of being parents, Dick and Jane didn't see the need to have holiday traditions for a being that would have no recollection of them other than what was captured forever in a photograph. When Joy turned two, however, the couple decided that it was time to make a plan.*
>
> *"Dick, remind me again what your family had for traditions." Jane started. "Well, my parents weren't really into traditions. Every year, our holidays seemed to change and we were at someone else's house all the time," he mused. "Looking back though, I wish we had SOME traditions."*
>
> *"It's settled then!" exclaimed Jane. We will make some traditions for Joy AND for you. What would you like our family Christmas traditions to be,*

honey?" Jane asked as the pen in her hand hovered with excited anticipation over a notepad. "I think I'd like to do the thing where you use powdered sugar to make Santa's handprints and footprints near the fireplace," he said as a boyish smile appeared on his face.

"Done!" Jane as she wrote it down. "I would like to incorporate one of my family's traditions of singing a few Christmas songs on Christmas Eve!" she continued as she made more notes on her paper.

Every Christmas from that moment on, Dick and Jane held to their new family traditions, and every year, they smiled at each other as they made a sugary mess on and around the fireplace knowing full well that their choices would inspire imaginative dreams in their little Joy.

Traditions are important to making memories as a family. The great thing about them is that you can make your own rules like you can with mythical creatures. All you must do is stick with them consistently, and that makes instant traditions. If your parents didn't have traditions, who cares? You aren't them; and you must do it for your children. There are no excuses, so if you don't have any, make some up, and suck less at traditions. Dream them up to be as weird, as fun, and as sugar filled as you like.

HER KIDS SAID

Mom: What is your favorite family tradition, and why?

Cabbage: (*Raises hand excitedly as he and his brother are wrestling on the couch*) Going on the field trip!

Mom: What?!

Cabbage: Going on field trips.

Mom: Road trips?

Cabbage: Yeah.

Mom: That's not a tradition. I'm talking about holiday traditions. Things we do at the holidays that we do every year.

Cabbage: Christmas!

Mom: That's not a tradition.

Cabbage: (*Raises hand excitedly again*) Halloween! On Halloween and Christmas, kids don't make cookies, but we make cookies.

Mom: Yes, the cookie-making is a tradition.

Cabbage: Yay!

Mom: Is that your FAVORITE tradition? The Halloween cookies. Is that your favorite?

Cabbage: (*Now lying across his brother's lap – stopped mid-wrestle*) About Halloween?

Mom: No, any holiday, all year.

Cabbage: Yeah. No. Yeah. I like the cookies on Halloween and Christmas.

Mom: Anthony?

Anthony: Same.

Mom: Okay. What is your second favorite holiday tradition, and why?

Cabbage: I don't know anymore.

Anthony: Presents!

Cabbage: That's not a tradition. Um… OOH! We, um, it's like Christmas day, we have to wait upstairs until you two are ready…

Mom: That's right.

Cabbage: And that's a tradition too. And, um, when we come downstairs, instead of just taking presents and ripping through that, we have breakfast, but instead of normal breakfast, it's toast and chocolate.

Mom: Oh yeah, that's good. I forgot about that actually. When you don't live with Mommy anymore, are there any of our family traditions that you would want to do with your family?

Cabbage: Ahhhh… cookie making and doing the thing I just said.

Mom: Chocolate toast?

Cabbage: Yeah, or anything chocolate.

Mom: Sit up. You guys are going to lose candy if you don't…

Anthony: Well, because it's so boring.

Mom: You're boring. Are there any traditions that you would change or add?

Both: (*Wrestling and making noises*)

Cabbage: What? I can't hear you. Anthony, get off me.

Mom: You guys aren't going to get treats…

Both: (*Straightening up*)

Cabbage: I want some.

Mom: Are there any traditions that you want to change or add… that we do or that you want us to do?

Both: (*Silence*)

Anthony: No. No, no.

Mom: You got nothin'? Okay, what do you think of the suet pudding that Grandma serves at Christmas at her house?

Cabbage: What's suet pudding?

Mom: That brown stuff that we put the sauces on… only at Grandma's house at Christmas. Everybody eats it. It's got raisins in it…

Both: I don't know what that is.

Mom: You guys haven't tried it?

Anthony: No. I don't think I even know what that is because I don't remember.

Mom: Your cousin calls it "sewer pudding"…

Both: No.

Any time I think about traditions from my childhood, I get the warm fuzzies. What great memories! When I think about the traditions I am making for my children, I hope that they will also look back someday with those same warm fuzzies. Traditions are part of what makes your family so unique and special.

Again, there are NO rules around what you can and cannot do to create your family traditions. The only limitation is your imagination and knowing that whatever it is that you decide on, you will need to continue to do it forever, so it should probably not be a huge chore or something you cannot afford to repeat.

The things we do for our kids, right? When they're little, and at the ages when they won't remember anything, the traditions are more for the parents... just like when you see a baby at Disney World. Why would you do that to yourself?! However, as the family grows together, and you get to enjoy the magic of the holidays as your kids are experiencing it, there is no better way to get some of those childhood warm fuzzies back than that.

Chapter 10:

It's Not Fair That Life Isn't Fair

M.O.M. SAID

We've all heard it from our parents: Life Isn't Fair. Growing up with an older sister, I remember hearing that line so many times when I asked for things she got before I did. Like so many of us, when we heard it, we didn't understand it and hated the logic. As a parent, however, I hear myself say this phrase so very often.

I have two same-sex children three years apart, so there's a lot of so-called "unfairness" due to birth order and age. We as adults know how unfair life is, but trying to convey that message to children who don't have the life experience to understand the gravity of it is practically impossible.

Any time I hear "That's not fair!" from one of my kids, I use that time to reiterate that nothing in life is fair:

- There will always be someone who has more than you.

- Your friend might get that video game because his parents don't have the same rules as I do.

- Your friend may have a phone, but you don't need a phone right now.

There's no way you're NOT going to have to counteract this line of protest if you have children. Parents of one child to parents of ten, we're all in the same pickle, and that pickle brine sure does stink! When reasoning and logic don't work as countermeasures, we always have this classic rebuttal to fall back on, "Because I said so." or "I'll think about it" which is parent speak for "I'm deferring this conversation in hopes that you forget about it."

One afternoon, when Jane was picking up Joy from school, Joy excitedly asked, "Mommy, can I get my ears pierced?" Unprepared for that question, Jane tried to defer her response by asking more questions, "Why do you want to do that?" "Well, Poppy just got her ears pierced, and her mom got her the prettiest little pony earrings, and I want them too!"

"Let me think about it," Jane grasped. "I will need to talk to your father about it first." Classic parent deferral method: needing time to speak to the other parent. "You know, Joy, I didn't get my ears pierced until I was a few years older than you are now." Jane reasoned, hoping to shut down the conversation.

As Joy crossed her arms, sunk in her seat, and overtly pouted, Jane realized that she needed to talk to Dick about how they would handle situations of unfairness as they moved ahead as a parenting team.

When they got home, Joy ran upstairs to continue pouting in her room, and Jane called her husband, "Dick, what are we supposed to do? She's so upset, and I tried telling her that I didn't get my ears pierced at that age." she explained. "Honey, we may just have to take a hard line with her," Dick said. "Well, I don't want her to think that she can use this logic with everything so I'm going to tell her that life just isn't fair. Are we on the same page then?" she asked Dick. "Yes, honey. I'll be home soon to back you up. I love you," he replied, good Dick that he was.

If you try to make life "fair" for your children, you'll set yourself up for failure. Sometimes I try to tie the unfairness logic into the peer pressure logic, hoping to prove that just because their friends are doing something, that doesn't mean that it's the right solution for everyone.

"So, if all of your friends jumped off a really high bridge, would you do it too?" I asked my oldest, Anthony when he whined again about how unfair life was because he didn't have a cell phone like his friends do. "Well, probably," he responded, debunking my whole plan to teach individual thinking and logic. Hmm... Guess my parenting is sucking a little in teaching effective countermeasures to peer pressure.

Could you imagine the idealized "fair" world that children believe could exist? What would that look like? It would be boring. Everyone would have the same life, the same things, the same job, the same face. We would be a society of boring ass clones. Life's not being fair is a testament to individuality and the freedom to make our own choices.

When your kids try to use the "it's not fair" complaint to you, try to use it to teach them about thinking for themselves, being a leader and not a follower... being the person who calls out to the other kids, "Don't follow them off the bridge!" Being unique in thoughts and actions sets you apart from the rest and is an admirable quality. The unfairness of life is just one more way for us to teach our children how to suck less.

HER KIDS SAID

Mom: Do you think that it is possible for everything in life to be fair? Why or why not?

Cabbage: (*Again more focused on holding the cat hostage*). Wait, what?

Mom: Do you think it's possible for everything in life to be fair? Why or why not?

Cabbage: Yes!

Anthony: Well, no, I don't think so.

Cabbage: No.

Mom: Why not?

Anthony: Because someone's older…

Cabbage: When someone's older, they get bigger stuff like less presents, but they get bigger stuff like when if you're a baby, you get baby toys, but you would be older, you would get play guns and depends if um, (*cat gets fed, up, and meows as she runs away*) like, I forgot what I was going to say, but…

Mom: What do you think is unfair that I'm holding you back from?

Cabbage: What do you mean?

Mom: Like when you say, "That's not fair!" because I say no to something, what is that circumstance where you're not getting what you want?

Cabbage: Ummmm... (*Looking at his brother*) you go first because I don't know anything of what you just said.

Mom: Let's talk about Roblox.

Cabbage: OOHHH!!!!

Both: (*Snickering*)

Mom: Why do you think that that's not fair... that I won't let you have Roblox?

Anthony: Bad. Influ – Ence.

Cabbage: Because they say a single bad word.

Mom: So, you think that I'm being unreasonable?

Cabbage: Like you can't even say M-E-A-T.

Mom: You think that I'm not letting you have something just to be mean?

Cabbage: (*Under his breath*) Well, you aren't mean.

Mom: You don't think I have a good reason... to fight with you about something? What is your logic in thinking that you need it for life to be fair? What is your argument for something needing to be fair?

Anthony: Nothing.

Mom: You have no argument, so you just say it to say it?

Anthony: I don't know.

Mom: Think about this now, if nothing was different for anyone in order for life to be completely fair, then everyone would have to be exactly the same: we would all look the same, act the same, have the same job, the same grades, the same amount of money, the same house... No one would be able to be unique and different because that wouldn't be fair. Does that sound like a world that you would want to live in?

Both: No!

Anthony: Zero percent.

Mom: So, the next time you say, "That's not fair", maybe do you think you might think about that?

Anthony: No!

Mom: Why not?

Cabbage: I think yes, because that was a good point.

Of course, I wish that life was fairer than it is, but back to my logic of how a truly fair life would be, that sounds boring. Without conflict, there can be no resolution. Without struggle, there can't be triumph. Without the depths of sorrow and sadness, the joy of happiness and bliss wouldn't be so great.

Have you ever noticed that people who seem to have the least stuff often have the most happiness and are the most content? Why do you think that is? The reason is that they have experienced the worst life has to offer, and that struggle has helped them to focus on what is truly important in life. If life had shown them 100% fairness, they would never have found the peace and happiness that they are fortunate to enjoy.

Until your children start to have struggles and triumphs in their own lives, it is our job as parents to talk through with them why life isn't fair and to put little hurtles in front of them so that they can learn how to jump over them the higher and higher they get as life goes on.

Chapter 11:

Stuff is Just Stuff, But Experiences Are the Gravity Bomb!

M.O.M. SAID

When your children are too little to do much other than be entertained as they poop and drool, you amass so much crap for them to look at, to touch, and to be read from. The smaller the child, the bigger the items that you purchase to keep them happy and entertained. As children get older, however, their wants become smaller and more expensive.

There also becomes a point when either you've run out of space in your home for more toys, or the only things your children want are too small and too expensive to make any sense, especially if you're trying to limit their screen time. I used to agonize about what "big" gift to get at birthdays and Christmas because one of my children never knows what he wants, and the other wants everything.

For as far back as I can remember, I've thrown them epic birthday parties. These parties are old-school, in-home, themed-to-the-max parties. We've had Army parties, fishing parties, at-the-beach parties, SpongeBob parties, police parties (with appearances by the actual police plus a police dog), Minecraft parties, and the last one was a made-up theme because I was throwing a combined party for a tween and a nine-year-old. "Rich in Chocolate" ... one of my greatest achievements in party planning. I bought a chocolate fountain, make up games to suit the theme, and purchased chocolate gold medals for game prizes, and full-sized candy bars for decorations.

I have been throwing combined birthday parties for the last nine years, and I have gotten away with it because both my kids are boys with birthdays in the same month but three years and three weeks apart. Because I was only spending money on one party, I rationalized that I could go all out and spend whatever I needed to make the theme amazing, but the chocolate-themed party was the last straw. I wasn't sure if I was going to make all that effort for myself or my kids, and the stress made me a b-witch. Several hundred dollars into the party planning, not including gifts, I thought to myself, "I think it's time to invest the party money into family vacations instead."

Earlier in the year before the party, we had taken the week of spring break to go on our first family road trip. The road trip was a gift from the prior year's combined birthday party, and I had been dreading it from the day I committed to the plan. How would the four of us survive fourteen hours in the car together? Would we all come back alive and unscarred? How would four people sharing a bedroom and a bathroom work out? How would I cut costs to make it affordable? Would we have enough room in the back of my SUV to fit all the crap we had to bring? Thinking about it was making me question why I'd decided to go on a road trip at all. After all, I'd been avoiding it for years, and it was a control freak's worst nightmare. I was sucking at having faith in my family and their ability to cohabitate for a week.

Regardless of the worrying and planning, the trip ended up a great success. Some of that success was a result of excellent planning on my part, combined with the right behavioral incentive milestones. Everyone was given a printed agenda at the start of the trip, and every day was broken down by time and stops with lunch and dinner plans called out and color-coded. The behavior incentives were phased up using the parent's trusty one-to-three system. Take a gander at a snippet of the agenda cut and pasted directly from the actual agenda document, with some details redacted for privacy:

1. **Day 1: Saturday, March 25 – TRAVEL DAY: Home -> Iowa**
    a. 8:00 am – leave the house
    b. Drive to (town), Iowa (7 hours)
    c. Check into (hotel name, city)
    d. <u>Behavior Incentives:</u>

  i. **0** *(highlighted in green)*: $5 Minecraft in-app purchase or $5 and pit stop travel treat

  ii. **1-2** *(highlighted in yellow)*: pit stop travel treat

  iii. **3+** *(highlighted in red)*: NOTHING

2. **Day 2: Sunday, March 26 – IOWA**

　a. Grandma's birthday

　b. Visit family

3. **Day 3: Monday, March 27 – TRAVEL DAY: Iowa -> Missouri**

　a. 9:30 am – leave the hotel

　b. (virtual check-in) Check into Hampton Inn Branson on the Strip

　c. Drive to **Lambert's Café** (1800 W. State Hwy J, Ozark, MO) 6.5 hours

　d. 4:30 Dinner at Lambert's Café *(green text)*

　e. Drive to Hampton Inn Branson on the Strip (40 minutes)

f. <u>Behavior Incentives:</u>
      i. **0** *(highlighted in green)*: $5 Minecraft in-app purchase or $5 and pit stop travel treat
      ii. **1-2** *(highlighted in yellow)*: pit stop travel treat
      iii. **3+** *(highlighted in red)*: No pool time tonight
4. **Day 4: Tuesday, March 28 - BRANSON, MO**
   a. 9:00 am – Titanic Museum (bring tickets)
   b. Lunch at the hotel
   c. Afternoon swim or explore
   d. **Dinner: Danna's BBQ and Burger Shop** *(green text)*

And so, the agenda continued to cover the whole weeks' worth of travel. We all had a good time, and none of us was smothered in our sleep with a pillow. Yes, there were hiccups like Cabbage kicking too much in his sleep and Anthony ending up on the floor, but kids remember things much differently than adults do. What did stupid me decide to do? I decided to do a mini road trip as a gift for their birthdays a few months later. "Please don't plan more than one family vacation in a year," my husband begged after the second road trip.

But I wanted to give experiences to my children instead of just things to pacify them and keep them busy but not engaged in the family. Of course, I took his plea to heart because he never asks for anything. However, I decided that for Christmas this year, I wanted to give another road trip to the boys. Just the one; it would replace the themed birthday party, and resources that would have been invested in another party would be put toward the trip.

Right now, it's fall, and I know I've made the right decision for my Christmas gift because Cabbage has told me four times since the mini trip that the next time we return to the amusement park, he wants to go to the water park. The future trip is to an all-inclusive water park, and I hate water parks, but parenting is also about sacrifice... to a degree.

When Joy was about eight, Dick found himself laid off from his high-earning job. Jane didn't make as much as Dick, and without his income, their household was struggling to make ends meet, let alone afford gifts for Joy's upcoming birthday. "I feel so bad, Jane," Dick started, "I feel like it's my fault that Joy won't get much for her birthday, and it's her golden birthday on top of that."

"Dick, don't beat yourself up. It's not your fault that the company made bad decisions and had to do layoffs," Jane empathized with Dick. "I'm sure we can still do something to make this birthday extra special for Joy. Try not to get so down about it." As she tried her hardest to think of an alternative, she scared Dick as she shouted, "I know! How about we take her to visit my cousin who just got that place on a lake about an hour from here. We can teach her how to catch frogs, well you can because eew, and we can teach her how to fish, and take her on boat rides, roast marshmallows over the fire. She would love that!"

Finally starting to perk up out of his funk, Dick agreed, "That's a great idea! Then we can celebrate with family too, and that will make her birthday extra special." Dreaming up the plans on a tight budget meant making a cake instead of buying a fancy one, but Joy and Jane made it together, and they laughed as they made the ugliest pony-shaped cake ever. They built forts in the woods, made marshmallow roasting skewers from sticks they found on a hike, and realized that they didn't need expensive stuff to provide happiness to their daughter on her special day.

While family vacations stress me out to no end, I can see the value in making those memories with my children. Even the few family vacations I took as a child, I remember with fondness: my parents falling asleep at a Disney World indoor water show, the muffler falling off about two hours into a very loud and clattery road trip, my mom throwing up on the side of the road in California because her friend was driving too fast around the curves. Good times.

Memories are memories – good, bad, funny, traumatic, but they stick with you. Stuff is just stuff that becomes clutter. If you can stomach it, I suggest trying a family road trip. Just don't forget to pack the headache meds and maybe some earplugs.

HER KIDS SAID

Both: (*Wrestling again on the couch*)

Mom: Stop! That's enough! We'll do the rest later… What is the best gift that you've ever received?

Both: (*Long period of silence*)

Mom: Oh, this is a tough one.

Both: (*Laughing*)

Mom: Why are you laughing? Does anyone have an answer for this? Best. Present. Ever.

Cabbage: New iPad.

Anthony: Ehhhh… I WAS GONNA SAY THAT!

Cabbage: Can't copy me.

Mom: What was your favorite birthday party theme, and why?

Anthony: The beach one.

Mom: Why?

Anthony: I like going to the beach.

Cabbage: Minecraft one because we got to have Minecraft toys.

Mom: Would you rather get a trip as a gift or a physical gift to play with or use?

Cabbage: Trip.

Anthony: What do you mean "a trip"?

Cabbage: (*As his brother is pushing on his face*) A family experience.

Anthony: Trip.

Mom: Why, Anthony?

Anthony: Probably because it's more fun than actually having stuff…

Cabbage: That can break easily.

Mom: PROBABLY more fun?

Anthony: Yeah, because we get to have a lot more fun with interesting stuff that we have never went to before.

Mom: What was your favorite part of the spring break trip to Branson, MO?

Both: (*Laughing*)

Mom: What was your favorite part?

Cabbage: Going to Silver Dollar City.

Anthony: Thunderation! (*a rollercoaster*)

Cabbage: … And… Time Traveler (another roller coaster), and having the funnel cakes.

Mom: Anthony, your favorite part?

Anthony: The swings and Thunderation probably? But maybe Time Traveler?

Mom: What did you think of the trip agenda I gave you? Did it help you to behave?

Cabbage: Yes!

Anthony: Yeah.

Mom: What did you think of the agenda?

Cabbage: I thought of it a lot of times because…

Anthony: Good!

Cabbage: Yeah!

Mom: And it helped you to behave then?

Both: Yep.

Mom: What was your least favorite part of the trip?

Cabbage: (*As his brother is playing drums on his lap*) Probably going on that bomb that went up…

Mom: Gravity Bomb?

Cabbage: Yeah, I hated that.

Anthony: I almost puked. I thought I fainted on that one.

Mom: You thought you fainted?

Anthony: Yeah, cuz I was like my stomach when I went down…

Mom: So, you both picked that as the worst part of the trip?

Both: Yeah.

Anthony: And probably the whole drivey…

Mom: The drive?

Anthony: Yeah, sucked.

Mom: (*As both kids are clearly getting anxious and fidgety*) Two more questions. What was your favorite part of the mini trip?

Anthony: What mini trip?

Mom: The Valleyfair (*amusement park*) trip.

Anthony: I loved going on the big swing. The tall thing that went like (*gestures moving in a circle while going upwards*)…

Mom: Yeah, that made me sick.

Cabbage: I almost fainted on that.

Anthony: No, you didn't.

Mom: What was your least favorite part of the mini trip?

Both: (*Silent from mental exhaustion and having to sit still for interviews*).

Anthony: Couple rollercoasters. Especially one that went straight down.

Cabbage: Uhhhhhhh… I don't know. I don't have one.

Mom: You guys kind of sucked at this round. That's why we have to stop.

Cabbage: Wait, um, I got a good one. When we went onto the first water ride…

Anthony: The one that spun around…

Mom: Thunder Canyon?

Anthony: In the tube…

Mom: Thunder Canyon.

Cabbage: Yeah, because that's the one I got mostly wet.

Anthony: I was the one that got the least wet, which was amazing (*smiling like he won some prize for getting the least wet*).

When I told the boys that we were taking another trip to Iowa for a family reunion the following year, Cabbage asked me excitedly, "Will you have the color-coded reward system for the car ride?" As a parent, I would have thought that my children would have hated having that system of checks and balances, but it's completely the opposite. They love knowing the boundaries and the rewards because the rules are very clear, and rewards are attainable and things they like.

Children thrive in structure and consistency. Being able to have achievable rewards is a great incentive to elicit good behavior, and a good behavior system is key to a successful family road trip.

As adults, we can fall into the trap of thinking that things can bring us happiness, and while they may be able to in the short term, it's the people and experiences we look back on with fondness. Being able to understand the value of experiences over stuff is a gift that not everyone will ever understand. However, when your children become old enough to enjoy experiences more than stuff, that's your opportunity to give them some of the best gifts that they and your family will ever receive.

Chapter 12:

It's Our Responsibility to Teach Responsibility and Respect

M.O.M. SAID

Money. There's either not enough of it or there's not enough of it. I can't say I've ever experienced having too much of it, but when it comes to money, most people fall into one of two categories: spenders or savers. For most of my life, I have been a hardcore spender. I can't help it. I love new clothes, shoes, and shiny things. Being a spender, I couldn't expect my children to grow up to be savers, could I? I would suck at parenting if I tried to apply the do-as-I-say-not-as-I-do logic to saving vs. spending.

About a year ago, I finally had an epiphany about my retirement and about saving vs. spending, and I'm a reformed spender. Mostly. I need to be a saver to be able to have a comfortable cushion because I'm on my own financially until my hubby retires, moves in, and we become a dual-income household. Finally, learning how to be a saver, I have been trying to teach my children the value of financial responsibility and hard work because I don't want them to have the rude awakening I wish I'd had sooner.

For years, I have been teaching my children responsibility when it comes to their things. They need to be responsible for picking up their messes, clearing their dishes, and keeping track of their winter gear and water bottles at school. All parents know how hard it is to avoid scouring the stinky mountain that is the lost-and-found area of the school.

Once my children finally mastered responsibility on the ground level, it was time to try to figure out a way to teach financial responsibility. Anthony is a natural saver. He thinks things over, and I'm proud of him for being a cheapskate. My littlest, Cabbage, will spend money as soon as it touches his fingers. I have created a chore system to aid in teaching responsibility. Each of my children has daily/weekly "to-do's" that are unpaid, like making their beds, clearing their dirty dishes and placing them in the dishwasher, putting their laundry away, and taking out the trash and recycling.

They each have a daily paid chore that needs to happen before we head off to school: my oldest cleans the litterboxes, and my youngest empties the dishwasher. Cabbage has dishwasher duty because he's the only person in the house besides me who knows where everything goes. From the items in the dishwasher that have unknown destinations, he makes a neat pile on the corner of the kitchen island. Sometimes, he even organizes the silverware drawer for fun or makes weird towers of clean dishes. For each week of chores, they are salaried at $2.00. Payday is the last day of the week at my house before they go to Dad's house, and they only get paid in full if they do their chores every. Single. Day. And I don't give out cash advances.

Being salaried employees starting at the very bottom, they also need to do "other duties as assigned". These duties are at the discretion of the employer me and consist of other chores they must do that are unpaid. Sometimes, there are opportunities for bonuses. My youngest likes to clean toilets for some reason. If he cleans all three, he gets an extra dollar. If he washes the floors, he gets two dollars. I have told them that if they ever want to earn more money, they can come to me with a proposal. If the snow falls from the roof onto the driveway and creates snow cement, they will get hazard pay for clearing that show with shovels because the snowblower has a hard time getting through it.

As an employer who pays starting wages, I am trying to teach them initiative, what it means to work hard for very little, and how to value money. If I paid them each $10.00 a week for doing something menial, they wouldn't value their money the same. "Mommy, I want to buy a $10 game add-on pack for my iPad game," says my youngest. "Do you know how long it takes you to earn $10 for doing chores? If you only earn $2.00 per week, and you're only here every other week; that means it takes you 10 weeks to earn $10. That's two-and-a-half months. Are you sure it's worth that to you?" To be perfectly honest, he doesn't seem to be getting it, but that's why he's only got a fraction of the amount of money his brother does.

The funny thing is that sometimes his brother recites my lines about the time it takes to earn money because he doesn't part with his so easily. When he had amassed a small fortune of $400, he asked me if he could get a bank account. If I wasn't at his birth, I'd question if he was my blood. After the three of us came home from our trip to the bank, I gave Anthony some play checks and told him that if he wanted to spend his bank money, he could write me a check. Seeing his brother doing adulty things made my youngest want to be a better saver. I still haven't been written a check almost a year later, and all the money remains intact at the bank... and is earning interest!

The other "R" that goes together with responsibility is respect. You can't teach responsibility without its brother, respect tagging along. Responsibility for other people's things and resources, like your parents' home and money, is a form of respect. Respect is also a hard concept to teach children.

"'Yes, Mommy,' is the correct response," I reiterate to them when I ask them to do something, and their initial response is "No", or "Do I have to?". I also make sure that they thank me for every meal I make or buy them or any meal that anyone else makes or buys them. "Thank you, Mommy, for dinner," I prompt as they clear their dinner dishes and wait for dessert. I don't even realize I'm saying it anymore because I've been saying it for so long in the same context over and over.

When my children and I are going anywhere, even if it's just coming back home, I encourage them to run ahead and hold the door open, "Go get the door for Mommy." This lesson happens mostly in the morning at drop off at the set of double doors to the elementary school, but I refuse to open the doors because they need to learn the art of respect and chivalry. Andy is a great role model for teaching chivalry because, without fail, he will open my car door before we all load up, and the boys see that. There is no better way to teach than to lead by example.

I know that these lessons are paying off because when they spend any time away from me, I get reports that they are the most polite, well-behaved, respectful children. On our family vacations, the ones that I made us take too many of this year, my children took it upon themselves to make their bed every morning in the hotel room. "Let's make our bed!" One proposed to the other as they happily worked together to undo the mess that had been made overnight.

> *Several months after Dick was laid off, he found a job that paid twice what he was making, and money was flowing freely in their house. They even told Joy that they would pay her for getting good grades. "Joy, for every A that you get, we will give you $50. Every B will earn you $20; anything beneath that gets nothing." Jane explained at the end of the first quarter as Joy's grades were starting to decline.*
>
> *With the new monetary incentive, Joy started making more of an effort, and when the end of the*

next quarter rolled around, she had earned herself enough money to buy the designer handbag she had been wanting. "Joy," Jane started, "You realize that if you buy that handbag, you won't have any money left over for anything else, and your next chance to earn money like that won't be for three more months," she warned, hoping that her tone would help make her point.

"Yeah, so what?" Joy snapped back as her finger hovered over the "Add to Cart" button on her phone. "I can make more money later" she continued as she finished the checkout process online. Jane shook her head and made a mental note to talk with Dick the next time they were home and alone.

"Dick, I think that we need to find a better way to teach Joy some responsibility," Jane whispered as they sat on the couch after Joy had gone to bed. "Why? What makes you say that?" Asked Dick. He listened as Jane explained what had happened earlier in the day, and he agreed that they needed a plan.

"We have more money now, but maybe that doesn't mean that we need to spend more. We are setting a bad example with our financial resources." Dick added. "You're right. I think maybe we need to stop paying her for grades and start having her earn money while also helping us out," Jane said. "Yeah, we are creating a monster, and we need to stop it. If she never has to work for what she has, she won't learn any respect or responsibility and will struggle in the real world," Dick said as Jane nodded.

That weekend, the couple sat down with their daughter for a family meeting and explained why they were changing the system and what was expected to earn money. "That's not fair!" Joy shouted. "Joy," Dick started, "Your mother and I have realized that we aren't doing you any favors by making it too easy for you to take things for granted. We want you to help around the house, and we will pay you accordingly. Oh, and life is never fair," he added.

Joy pouted for a week, and she didn't help around the house, but since both Dick and Jane stood firm in their resolve to hold Joy to the new standard, Joy eventually started to work hard to earn the money she wanted. Since she wasn't making very much compared to the amount of work, she learned that she needed to save longer to be able to afford life's shiny new rewards. When she finally rebuilt her money to afford a new handbag, she decided that she had worked too hard and too long to spend it on something she didn't even need.

The trash bag story is one of my proudest moments in teaching responsibility and respect. I was in the kitchen, as I often am, and I was pulling out a full bag of trash from the bin. "I'll take the trash out!" I heard from upstairs as Cambridge excitedly hustled downstairs to the kitchen. "How did you know I needed the trash taken out?" I asked with confusion. "I heard the trash bag from upstairs." I stood there dumbfounded with a goofy grin on my face for a good five minutes as he quickly scrambled to put his shoes on and raced off toward the end of the driveway with the trash bag thrown Santa-style over one shoulder.

Not only did he take the initiative to help without being asked, but he also took joy in being able to help me out, and he's only nine. I'm excited about the kind of person he will grow up to be!

Parents give and give and give, and it only takes one moment, like the trash bag incident, to tell us we're on the right track and doing a good job. Most of the time, I just need to set a full trash bag by the back door, and it disappears. Sometimes they even fight over who will get to take it to the end of the driveway to the trash bin.

In parenting, unlike in the workplace, there's no one to give us a review and a raise for a job well done or for going above and beyond. We get those raises and accolades in those unexpected moments of our children offering their assistance, and they are so much more meaningful than the biggest raise could ever be.

HER KIDS SAID

Mom: Let's finish this one, and then you can pick out a candy reward... What do you think it means to be responsible?

Cabbage: Oh, um, responsible means being responsible for your items... like, you don't lose 'em, you don't break 'em, you be gentle with them. Like say, I had this (picks up his brother's iPad). You have to be responsible with it. You don't wanna be like (gestures slamming down his brother's iPad), or (swings the iPad sideways like he's going to hit someone in the face with it).

Mom: Anthony, what does it mean to you?

Anthony: (Slumped over onto the armrest of the couch because he's so done with book interviews) Same thing. Pretty much.

Mom: Okay, Anthony gets to answer first. What do you think it means to be respectful?

Anthony: You have to be polite. Being polite means not to be rude to other people, and help other people out who need it. Or just help them out if they didn't ask for it.

Cabbage: Um, be polite… wait, what was the question again?

Mom: What do you think it means to be respectful?

Cabbage: You wanna be nice, you wannabe polite, you wanna be like um, yeah, I forgot.

Anthony: You just said the same thing that I did.

Mom: Do you think that your two dollars a week for chores is fair?

Cabbage: Yes.

Anthony: (Mumbles into a couch pillow) Pretty much.

Cabbage: I do.

Mom: In what circumstance do you think it makes sense to spend more than twenty dollars of your own money, taking into consideration that twenty dollars is roughly five months of chores, which is almost half a year?

Cabbage: Not worth it.

Mom: When do you think that it would make sense to spend twenty dollars of your own money?

Cabbage: Never.

Mom: You did at the Titanic Museum.

Cabbage: Well, that was from the birthday party. That wasn't my own money; that was from the birthday party.

Mom: That was gift money. And that's different?

Cabbage: Yeah, not my own money.

Mom: So, you wouldn't spend twenty dollars of your earned money?

Cabbage: Hmmm (mumbles) I should have kept my money.

Mom: Yes, you should have. What about you, Anthony?

Cabbage: (Butting in defensively) I love the Titanic, okay!?

Anthony: I would spend it on stuff I like.

Mom: Like what?

Anthony: I don't know.

Mom: You would spend five months of work's pay on something you like?

Cabbage: (Interrupting) on Minecraft.

Anthony: No, not Minecraft.

Mom: What do you do when you see a full trash bag by the back door?

Cabbage: Take it out.

Mom: Why?

Cabbage: Because I just do it because it feels right.

Mom: Didn't you say yesterday something about how you do it because you're bored sometimes?

Cabbage: Yeah, because I'm bored, maybe I'm mad and I gotta get that STEAM out!

Mom: Anthony, when I put a garbage bag by the back door, what do you think?

Anthony: Well, he's already gonna do it, so there's no point in doing it.

Mom: Well, what if you guys are outside, and I set it outside?

Anthony: (Groans) I don't know.

Cabbage: I probably do it.

Anthony: I don't even get a chance. He just grabs it like it's his, so… I couldn't do it anyways.

Mom: Why do you then take the garbage without being asked?

Both: (Silence)

Cabbage: (Hits his brother with the back of his hand) You go, Anthony. I can't stop staring.

Mom: Why would you do something like that without being asked?

Cabbage: Becaaaaaauuusseeee... um, because I wanna be nice. And I want to be polite so you don't have to do it. And you said to me, um, to be like, do it right away because usually we don't do it right away. Like mostly when you take out the garbage, it's mostly at dinner, and you say, "Can you take the garbage out when you're done?" I just get my shoes on and take them out right away.

Mom: Because it's better to do something now than later?

Cabbage: Yeah. And plus, it's better when you've got hot food because it's like you don't want to burn your mouth, so instead of just waiting there blowing on it, you could just go and do something quick and then come back and your food would be cooled. Like yesterday I did that.

Mom: Your food would be too hot?

Cabbage: Yea, it started hot, and I blew on it, and it was still steaming, so I took out the garbage right away and I went outside, and when I came back in, it was cold.

Mom: The right temperature?

Cabbage: Yeah.

Responsibility and respect are our responsibility to teach as parents. It's about setting up your child for success in the future in a way that you can maintain, enforce, and keep consistent. Muscle memory, remember? If you keep up a system and don't deviate from the guidelines set forth by either party, eventually, your child will fall in line with their expectations. Will it be easy? No. Nothing in parenting is easy, except maybe loving them. But you didn't go into parenting, assuming that it would be easy.

Here's an extreme example of my children's respect for my home. They are so well-trained about not wearing their shoes on my floors that if they've already put their shoes on but need to get something in the kitchen, they do this weird knee-walk-crawl across-the-floor thing to get to whatever it is that they need. They will not, under any circumstance, wear their dirty shoes on my floors. It's fantastic, but somehow, my floors still end up dirty. Oh well, Cabbage likes to wash floors!

After the trash bag story happened, Cabbage surprised me with a parenting gift of sorts. It was a school day, and I was upstairs in my bathroom, putting my makeup on. My phone chimed, indicating an instant message:

Cabbage: Can I take out the garbage (trash bin emoji)

Cabbage: Plz

Me: Yes, and can you put the trash bin out at the end of the driveway? It's just trash, not recycling. Thank you!

Cabbage: Ok

After he had made multiple trips to take out two heavy bags of trash and a dirty furnace filter, he came into my bathroom and asked if the large rectangular item (the furnace filter) was trash or recycling. "It's trash. Why? Did you put it in the recycling?" I asked. "I'll be right back," he said as he raced off to brave the cold, dark November morning. My littles know that they don't get money or treats for taking out the trash, and there was my nine-year-old begging to take out the trash. That's how you know you're doing a good job as a parent teaching initiative, responsibility, and respect.

Here's what it comes down to, if you don't want to end up with spoiled rotten monsters, you need to suck less at teaching responsibility and respect. Your kids will either learn it from you, or they won't learn it until the world teaches them. If the world is their teacher, the lessons will be harder with bigger, more negative life-changing consequences.

When children are little sponges, we as parents can set our children up for success, but teaching respect and responsibility often means enacting tough love and battling some epic tantrums. If you choose to soft parent your way through these times, your children will end up paying for it, literally and figuratively.

Chapter 13:

Life Skills 101

M.O.M. SAID

Decades ago, when family values seemed to be a little more prevalent and substantial, it was a no-brainer that children would be taught life skills by their parents: cooking, organization, laundry, money management, respect, changing a tire, mowing... all the black-and-white TV show kinds of things plus other critical skills for success. These days, parents seem to have less time or less motivation to teach the classics. After all, it is hard to teach your children to cook if you can't cook.

> *One of the things that Jane liked to do on the weekends was bake, and she loved teaching Joy how to do what she enjoyed. One Saturday afternoon, after coming home from an appointment, Jane*

walked into the house to the smell of sweet, chocolatey goodness.

"Who is baking?" she asked, confused. As she turned the corner and entered the kitchen, she saw Joy teaching her dad how to bake her favorite chocolate chip cookies. "What's going on here?" she asked, still not believing what she was seeing. Dick hardly ever set foot in the kitchen unless he was foraging for a snack, sneaking bites as dinner was being prepared, or doing dishes.

"I'm teaching Daddy how to make something nice for you, Mommy," Joy explained in a proud voice. "Sorry for the mess, dear," Dick apologized. "Don't worry about it. How did you know how to make my favorite cookies, Joy?" Jane asked as she stood surveying the heaps of dishes and spills of ingredients. "You taught me, remember?" Joy said as she scooped a warm cookie onto a cooling rack.

It was at that moment that Jane realized she was inadvertently teaching her daughter a life skill, and that interaction inspired her to speak with Dick about how they could make sure that they taught their daughter more skills so that she could become the independent woman that they wanted her would be.

Life skills are the basics of living alone that we need to teach our children so that they can move out confidently and successfully into the world beyond our homes. Here are some of the life skills that I am working on with my children that you can work on alongside me:

<u>*Life Skill 1: Cooking*</u>

Cooking is one life skill that is quickly becoming lost. Why? So many parents sign their kids up for so many sports or activities that there is no time to cook. As a person who could not suck more at sports (I could be standing one foot away from a trash bin and miss the shot), I don't feel the need to push sports too hard on my children. While I see some value in them, I do not value them at the loss of other crucial family values and skill sets. Skillsets that can be learned in other ways.

My Grandparents lived across the street from us when I was little, and my Grandma was always cooking, baking, cleaning, or ironing. I didn't learn until after she'd passed that she had never gotten her driver's license. With a fair amount of child-like naivete, I just assumed that she liked to do all those things, not that she was essentially tethered to the house. On the other hand, my mother didn't do a lot of cooking from scratch, and when she did, they were simple meals. Because my parents owned a small-town grocery store & gas station, they hardly ever had time to do anything other than sleep or work. Despite being positively influenced by two amazing women, my grandmother or my mother did not teach me cooking or baking skills.

How did I become such a great home chef aficionado? When I got married to my first husband, I was two weeks out of graduating from college. While I didn't make a great deal of money whilst still being in my first internship, we were still classified as DINK: Dual Income No Kids. When you don't have to cook, and you have disposable income, you go out... a lot. I loved going out to eat after a long day at work, and I still love going out, but there came a time when it wasn't a financially responsible option anymore. I needed to suck a lot less at cooking. But how?

After a few years of marriage, I started my own business and was working from our two-bedroom townhouse. Working from home was amazing until my husband got a work-from-home job too, and the townhouse shrank to the size of a pinhead. When we moved to a big four-bedroom + office house with an attached three-car garage and a tiny yard, our house payments didn't allow for our restaurant dinner lifestyle.

What to do...? I had to learn to cook. My husband got me a ridiculous cooking video game, but it sparked my interest in cooking. I remember the first dinner I made for my first husband's parents when they came to visit: eggplant parmesan. As I sat down at the table and proudly served the dinner, I jokingly said, "Well, it's the first time I've made this, and I'm learning to cook." My mother-in-law said, "Well, if it's bad, at least there's an Arby's down the street." "That's not very nice!" her husband scolded.

I honestly cannot remember if the dish was good or bad. Regardless, I'll never forget the trepidation that I served that meal with, the commentary, or the humble cooking beginnings that started my journey to becoming the "best restaurant in town" according to my children and second husband, Andy. Andy always tells me that he never liked food before I met me. That's high praise, and I'll take it!

Knowing what I know now about the importance of knowing how to cook, I have assigned myself the task of making sure my children know how to. Presently, my kitchen rules allow my oldest to deal with stovetop things like browning ground beef. He's my sous chef. My youngest is precise but too young to deal with fire, so he's either my prep cook, kitchen boy, or pastry chef, depending on the need. Everyone in the house also has their own apron, which must be worn when working in Mommy's kitchen.

At this point, Anthony can make scrambled eggs for himself with no help. He cracks and whisks eggs, preheats and sprays the pan, cooks the eggs, tops them with cheese and salt, and then puts all of the dirty dishes in the dishwasher. Mommy no havie to makie lunch! I LOVE that. I'm not a my-child-is-getting-too-old-too-fast kind of mom. I'm the I-love-seeing-them-mature-

and-evolve-and-cheer-from-the-sidelines kind of mom.

Yes, there were times when they were younger when they would ask if they could help, and I had neither the time nor the patience to teach them. However, setting aside my control-freak time management nature, I have learned patience through teaching them a skill set that they and I will be proud of. My goal is that before they move out of my house, they will be making dinner while I relax on the couch after work! Sounds like heaven to me.

Life Skills 2 & 3: Changing Oil and Mowing the Yard

Andy is working on a plan to teach the boys how to mow the lawn and change the oil in our vehicles. Having changed the oil in every one of his vehicles for his whole life and being the one to fix his cars, he sees the value in mechanical knowledge and believes it to be a skill that everyone should have. Both of us are excited for the day; they have enough height and power to push the snowblower because winters suck in Duluth!

Life Skill 4: Organization

The life skills of tidiness and organization are also ones that I find valuable to instill in my children. Messes and clutter make me anxious, and little "particulates" on my kitchen floors drive me insane. Each of my children has a different filing vs. piling mentality. My oldest Anthony is a minimalist and doesn't seem to like clutter. His little brother, however, hates to throw anything away. To his credit, Cabbage saves things because he has a creative vision for a future project.

They clean their rooms regularly, purging unwanted items regardless of their organizational preferences. The last time Anthony purged his room, I hadn't even asked. I just saw a pile of misfit items outside of his room. "What is that pile of stuff?" I inquired. "I don't want that stuff in my room anymore," he explained. His brother then foraged for the items he wanted, and the rest was put in the trash.

By keeping my house organized and clean, I am working to provide a tidy and organized environment. An environment without clutter encourages kids to do the same with their own spaces. Life skill learned! Yay us.

Life Skill 5: Time Management

Effective time management is one of the most important life skills you can teach your children. Unfortunately, you cannot teach this skill effectively if you suck at it. I'm of the mindset that if you're on time, you're late, and there's no time like the present to do things.

When I pick my children up from school, one of the first things I ask is, "Do you have any homework?" Homework is required to be completed before dinner for multiple reasons:

1. It's smart to do homework first because it's an important and high-priority item. Learning to prioritize is key to effective time management.

2. If they need help with homework, my brain stops functioning after dinner time.

On Fridays, I give them a choice to do their homework on Friday or over the weekend, but I always say, "If you get it done now, you'll have the whole weekend free, NOT to do homework. Doesn't that sound like a good idea? If I were you, I would do the homework now because it's better to do it and get it over with." For the most part, unless it's a big project or multiple subjects worth of homework, they choose wisely and get it done on Friday.

Life Skill 6: Harness the Power of the List

I do so love lists: in the bathroom, on the sofa table, on the kitchen counter, on my phone, on my desk at work, on my desk at home, on my refrigerator... and the lists go on! Lists, in conjunction with my Google calendar, are what keep my life on time, on task, and running smoothly and efficiently.

While I may not be able to transform my husband into an effective list-maker and user, I am determined to teach my children this critical life skill. Anthony was recently invited to his first sleepover, and instead of making a list and packing for him, I sat down with him and had him go through the process of writing his packing list.

"Think through your day and what you need at different times of the day as you think about what you will need to pack," I instructed with more patience than I usually have. "Now, make each thing a different line item so you can cross them off as you pack them. What do you need when you are getting ready for bed?" I asked. "My toothbrush, toothpaste, and my pajamas," he responded. After having him think through his day and other scenarios like getting dirty, playing outside and needing an extra change of clothes, I cross-checked his list with the one I keep in my "Lists" folder on my computer.

After he made his list, he oversaw packing himself and putting the handwritten list in the packed bag. If he did the packing from a list he made, he would remember what he packed when it was time to come back to my house. If he was struggling to remember what he brought, he could refer to the list that he packed. The list to come back home isn't a list I use, but for a child who seems to misplace and forget things, it's a best practice for him.

Life Skill 7: Work Smarter, Not Harder

As I type this sub-headline, I can hear my dad's voice in my head saying this mantra. It's hard not to want to shake my head and roll my eyes because that was my snap reaction whenever he said it. What the heck was he talking about in his cryptic dad-speak? Whatever it was, it sank in so much that it came out the other side... out of my mouth in the direction of my children.

Working harder and not smarter is one of my favorite skills because it is essentially finding the most efficient way to do something, and I love efficiency so much. If I could have married it, I would have! There's no way I could accomplish all that I do without finding ways to work smarter and not harder. Cabbage gets it. Every time he finds a way to work smarter, he tells me, "Work smarter, not harder, right Mommy?" Music to my ears.

The caveat to teaching life skills to your children is that you must have mastered that life skill first.

It's not a case of those who can't do, teach. Those who can do, need to teach. I don't want my children to go out into the world completely unprepared; I want them to step confidently out on their own paths. I also don't want them living in my basement until they're forty.

HER KIDS SAID

Mom: Do you think it's better to do your Friday homework on Friday or on Saturday or Sunday, and why?

Both: Friday!

Mom: Why?

Cabbage: Because then you don't have to do it on the weekend, so you just have like, a GOOD weekend. You don't have to do any math; you could just relax and do anything you want instead of doin' math the whole two days.

Mom: Anthony?

Anthony: Uh, it would be… what is it, what's the words? It would be… You would be more on top of homework so you wouldn't have like a ton of homework, and then you would have to do it all on Saturday and Sunday. It would be better if you get it done before it's like late or something.

Mom: (*Cabbage starts hitting himself on the leg with the end of a phone charger cord*) Cabbage. Stop that. Can you describe to me the last time you worked smarter, and not harder?

Both: (*A long silence*)

Mom: You just said this to me yesterday.

Anthony: I don't even know.

Cabbage: (*Sunk into the couch*) I forgot.

Mom: You got nothin'? No instances of remembering to do something smarter and not harder? (*Cabbage resumes hitting himself in the leg with the phone charger cord*). I think it had something to do with your gloves last night, but I don't remember what.

Cabbage: (*Makes a sad, quiet whining sound*)

Mom: Please don't play with that.

Cabbage: Why?

Mom: You know what it means though, right? To work smarter, not harder, right?

Cabbage: Like instead of like when you refill the corn for the animals outside, and instead of bringing one at a time, you bring all three and stack them... I bring all three, and I stack them up. Then I separate all three, fill them up, and then stack them up and go like (*gestures putting out the bowls by un-nesting them*) boom, move on, then boom, move on, and then boom. Done.

Mom: That's exactly right. What kinds of skills do you think you'll need to have before you leave to live on your own?

Anthony: I didn't even hear none of that.

Mom: What are you going to need to do before you move out and...

Cabbage: Um, cook, do dishes...

Anthony: Obviously drive (*laughs anxiously*).

Cabbage: Drive, keep the house clean, turn on the TV, (*mumbles*) I don't know how to do that. Um, uh, clean...

Anthony: Pay your bills.

Mom: What else do you see me doing all the time?

Cabbage: Do the laundry.

Mom: Yeah.

Anthony: That's painful.

Cabbage: Do the um, fold clothes, um, keep the house clean…

Anthony: (*Annoyed*) you just said that.

Cabbage: Oh, I did.

Mom: What about the stuff outside?

Anthony: Well, no. I thought you meant in the house.

Mom: No, just living on your own.

Anthony: You would live in an apartment, and then you would live in a house.

Mom: I mean, like mowing…

Anthony: Oh.

Mom: Snow blowing…

Anthony: Shoveling...

Cabbage: Ooh, Ooh, wait! Um, cut down branches that are like hanging…

Mom: Yard maintenance…

Anthony: Work. All. Day. Every day of your life.

Mom: What are you good at now, and how will that help you when you live on your own?

Cabbage: I'm good at putting away the dishes.

Mom: That's right.

Cabbage: (Points to his forehead) Remembering!

Anthony: I don't think I'm going to have a cat anyways, so... (*His chore is cleaning the litterbox*)

Mom: What are you good at though, now? Just in general, that will help you... any of those things that you guys listed.

Cabbage: I know that I'm good at keeping organized. That's a good skill.

Anthony: No, you're not.

Cabbage: Yeah, I am.

Mom: Anthony, you're not good at anything that you can transfer as a life skill right now?

Cabbage: Take out the garbage and recycling and do it fast. (*Pauses*) I don't think that's a skill. Is this a skill where you take a pill without water... wait, no, that isn't a skill. Oh, it might be, actually.

Anthony: No, it isn't.

Cabbage: Taking a pill without using water, just your spit, maybe.

Mom: (*Laughs*)

While I certainly would never try to teach the skill of ironing to the point, my grandmother did it – ironing my Grandpa's boxers, pillowcases, and sheets – I find it to be a necessity in parenting to teach our children the basic skills that they need for them to be successful on their own. Making time to teach your children life skills will require patience and repetition. If you want your child to learn something that neither you nor your partner excels at, then it's a great opportunity to learn as a family. Bonus: lesson learning also counts as a family experience and a memory.

Opportunities to teach your children life skills can present themselves in multiple instances throughout your week. Oftentimes, you can multitask a chore while also teaching your child life skills and responsibility. Efficiency – OOH yes! I'll take more of that, please.

If you can teach your child the skill of helping to clean, they can help you out, they can learn respect for your home, and you can use that opportunity to teach them about financial responsibility if they are paid for that chore. Doesn't that make you excited to be able to do all those things at once?.

Chapter 14:

Fireside Chats Minus the Fire

M.O.M. SAID

The "fire" in my house is electric and controlled by a remote, and our chats aren't by it, but we do have frequent little conversations (or what the business world calls "fireside chats") about life. My family fireside chats are just any in-the-moment chance that I get to teach my children a life lesson. Many of our abbreviated conversations happen on the twelve-minute ride to the school from the house or the school back to the house. Twelve minutes is approximately the length of a child's attention span for learning a life lesson anyway, and they're a captive audience in the car.

When I went through a year of interviewing for a new job, I gave my children real-time updates. I explained to them why I was looking for a new job, expressed to them what goes into preparing for those interviews, and asked them to wish me luck before each interview. I used my life experience to teach them that you should always strive to achieve the highest level possible and that if you aren't being appreciated in your job, you should find an employer that values you. I was also trying to teach them that you should study hard for an interview and that you should try your hardest to be respectful of the interviewer's time while also giving the best first impression of yourself.

They've seen me cry when I made it to the final round and lost out to the other candidate, but they also saw me pick myself up and keep trying. Through the roller coasters of my emotions, I talked to them about what drives me forward, why ambition is important, and how we are not a family of quitters.

More recently, our conversations have swirled around what they want to be when they grow up. I wish someone had enlightened me earlier on some of the more obscure career paths that exist...

like the one I have now. I had never heard of someone being a Director of Development until I applied for this job. Why didn't I know that there are more careers than a doctor, lawyer, astronaut, or police officer? Well, there is a police officer in this family so that career path is a highlighted option.

In kicking off the conversation early about careers, I want them to start to identify their strengths and what kinds of things they are interested in. The more they learn to express those interests, the more options I can talk to them about in terms of career paths. The wrench in the career path conversation is artificial intelligence. I find myself warning them to steer clear of careers that computers and/or robots will take over. It's a weird reality, I know.

At this point, I am encouraging my youngest to go into the medical profession, specializing in something like becoming a medical examiner or a coroner. He watches the gross reality shows with me about autopsies and blemish squeezing, and when Andy says he saw a dead body at work, Cabbage's first thought is, "What did it look like?!"

Anthony, my oldest, well, I think he may be suited for a trade. Something not in an office or at a desk. He needs to do something with his hands or body to stay focused, and the trades are becoming lost arts that are now in high demand and paying very well. There's no shame in a blue-collar profession. I've married different colors of collars, and the color of someone's metaphorical collar is no reflection of the size of their heart or the depth of their character.

"I want to be a storm chaser!" exclaimed Anthony during a thunderstorm. He's completely obsessed with the weather. He even calls me from his dad's house to tell me when there's a storm warning or lightning strike nearby. It's cute. "Anthony," I cautioned, "There are some things that might be better hobbies than careers... like storm chasing. Maybe that could be a hobby. You want a job with good benefits like health insurance and a retirement plan." Oh. My. Gosh, I am becoming my father... the father I thought I had nothing in common with. "Maybe

I'll be a meteorologist then," he corrected. That's why these career discussions are important: to get them thinking about and weighing their options.

> *Joy's friend Poppy moved a few houses down the street from Joy, and the two couldn't have been happier. Because of the proximity, Jane offered to pick up Poppy on their way to the school in the morning. On one particularly tough morning, Joy woke up on the wrong side of the bed. She hadn't slept well and was just looking to start a fight about anything with anyone.*
>
> *When Poppy got into the back seat next to Joy, Poppy's backpack blocked Joy's heat vent, and the car hadn't had a chance to warm up yet in the frigid temperatures. Grabbing Poppy's backpack with a swift and careless gesture, she threw it onto her friend's lap and spewed, "I'm cold, and you put your backpack over my heat vent!"*
>
> *"Joy! Is that any way to talk to your best friend?" Jane scolded. "Maybe you should have said, 'I am cold, but your backpack is blocking my heat vent. Would you mind if I moved your backpack to the*

back where you can still grab it when it's time for you to get out of the car?' Don't you think that commentary would go over better with your friend than just grabbing her backpack and yelling at her for putting it in a place that she normally puts it?"

Immediately realizing how rude she was from her mother's comments and the look on her friend's face, Joy apologized. When Jane picked up Joy from school that afternoon, she again talked to Joy about effective communication when Joy was in a better mood to have a rational discussion.

With my oldest knocking on the door of metamorphosizing into a teenager, we have had to broach more complicated topics. He came home one day with an invitation to a birthday party from a friend at school whom he's not allowed to be friends with. I don't enjoy these kinds of discussions at all, but they must be done. "She's a bad influence... falling asleep in class, not doing her homework, getting suspended. You can be nice to her in school, but I don't want you to be friends with her." I explained.

"But my other friends are going," he quietly protested. "Anthony, I wanted to give you the opportunity to make the right decision, but when you don't, it's my job as your parent to step in. Friends at this age can lead you down a path to nowhere, and I won't let it happen." I explained to him how my sister had some of those friends and how those friends helped steer her off course.

I'm not sure if the reason he wanted to go was that his other friends were going or that he wanted to be friends with her, but I told him, "Allowing you to hang out with her outside of school is fostering a friendship that I don't approve of." Sometimes parenting downright sucks, but you deal with the hard stuff when your kids live at home so that their lives don't suck as much when they grow up.

HER KIDS SAID

Mom: We are doing the next one.

Anthony: Well, I didn't have anything for that one.

Mom: It's fine if you don't have an answer. What do you want to be when you grow up?

Cabbage: (*Raises hand*) Done! The people who cut up dead bodies and see how they died.

Anthony: (*Laughs*) I don't know.

Cabbage: Brah!

Mom: Didn't we have a whole conversation about this?

Anthony: It would be fun to be a tree chopper. You go up a tree, cut down the branches, and cut the whole thing up. That'd be fun.

Mom: What do you think…

Cabbage: Like a lumberjack?

Anthony: No, you don't use an axe. You use a chainsaw the whole time.

Mom: What do you think might be the benefits of a job you pick?

Cabbage: What does that mean?

Mom: What are the good reasons to do that job?

Anthony: It's fun. It's better than sitting at a desk and doing nothing.

Cabbage: Uh, wait. You get paid a lot of money? I don't know.

Mom: That's exactly the answer I was looking for.

Cabbage: Oh.

Mom: What might be some of the issues with the job that you just picked?

Anthony: In the winter.

Cabbage: (*Raising his hand*) Ooh, I know! When, like the power goes off…

Mom: How is that a bad thing?

Cabbage: Well, there's like that machine where like it keeps people alive when you take out the heart. That could be an issue, or if I'm workin' downstairs, and that happened, and the power goes off…

Mom: Wait, wait, wait. So, are you dealing with dead bodies in your job or live people?

Cabbage: Dead people.

Mom: So then why does it matter if the power goes off?

Cabbage: I don't know. Well, if like… is there like a machine that can easily cut open dead bodies?

Mom: A saw and a scalpel.

Cabbage: No, that needs electricity.

Mom: Yeah…

Cabbage: A chainsaw?

Mom: Sort of. A bone saw.

Cabbage: What the heck?!

Mom: Okay, anyway…

Cabbage: That's cursed!

Mom: So that's the issue?

Cabbage: Yeah, if the power went off.

Mom: You don't think that maybe… okay yours is working outside in the snow?

Anthony: Yeah, that would suck (*laughs*).

Cabbage: That was a good one.

Mom: Do you think that if I, as your mother, think you shouldn't do something you want to do, I have a good reason that I said no?

Cabbage: Yeah, you always have good reasons so I would not do it.

Anthony: Even though we say we want to do it so bad? Um, no

Cabbage: What'd you say?

Mom: The question was, "If I tell you that you shouldn't do something that you want to do, do you think I have a good reason…"

Both: Yes.

Anthony: Didn't know what you meant, but yeah.

Mom: Okay.

Cabbage: I've always wanted for Christmas a present with loom bands.

Mom: Okay, stop playing with the cord; you're gonna break it. What would you do if you were a parent, and your child was about to make a mistake, but they didn't know it?

Cabbage: (*Making binoculars with his hands in front of his eyes*) Wait, what?

Mom: If you were a parent, and your child was about to make a mistake, but they didn't know it, what would you do? Would you let them make the mistake, or would you step in, and stop it from happening?

Both: Stop it from happening!!

Cabbage: It depends on what kind of mistake though.

Mom: So that's why I say "no" because I know…

Cabbage: Like if I wet your pants.

Anthony: Depression of killing yourself.

She: Okay, that's dark. I'm just saying, that's the reason why I say "no" because I know you're about to make a mistake.

Anthony: (*Pretends to push his brother over in slow motion as Cabbage makes an exploding sound effect. I'm losing them.*)

Mom: Anthony! Do you think that it made sense why Daddy and I wouldn't let you go to you-know-who's birthday party at the movie theater? Do you think it makes sense why we said "no"?

Anthony: Well, obviously I know NOW, cuz I used to watch it, and it wasn't scary at all, but now they changed it, and now it is…

Mom: So now we are talking about the movie they were going to for the birthday party and not the person that you were going to be hanging out with?

Anthony: Well, the person isn't that great, but she isn't the worst.

While Cabbage always knows where his things are, my oldest struggles to remember details because he is in "Anthony Land". One morning, after we dropped Anthony off at the middle school, his brother stated, "He's going to forget to bring his gym clothes home." After I had just shouted the reminder as Anthony walked away from the car. Seeing a moment to teach a little two-minute lesson, I told Cabbage that when we realize we have shortcomings, we need to devise a system to compensate for them so that we don't need someone else to manage our lives.

His older brother had just started a new system of cataloging his day on a sticky note in his binder, and it was starting to help him keep track of what homework he had, what tests he had coming up, etc. That day's note had a byline to remember to bring home his gym clothes. "You have to retrain your brain to work with the system you put in place to compensate for anything you're not great at, and the sooner that you can do that, the easier your life will be," I explained to him as we pulled into the elementary school.

Using little parcels of time, even a few minutes, to multitask and teach lessons in the moment is an efficient and effective way to up your parenting game. Every action can teach a lesson, and when you have a captive audience, you need to take advantage of those opportunities. If, in those moments of captivity, you find yourself without a fireside chat to chat about, you can always use that time to get to know your children a little bit better; you might be surprised or amused by their answers.

Chapter 15:

Please Use Good Manners and Etiquette. Thank You.

M.O.M. SAID

Please, thank you, yes ma'am, yes sir. When was the last time you heard any of these phrases from a child... a child in real life? Before I decided to have children, my first husband and I were visiting his older sister in Arizona. Her little kids were playing in a tiny pretend kitchen, and I heard them exchange pleasantries with each other as they played. I told him that if I did ever have children, I would want them to be polite just like that. I'd never witnessed such a thing before. They weren't behaving like the little monsters I thought most kids were.

Very recently, at fourth-grade parent-teacher conferences, Cabbage's teacher made it a point to tell us that she highlighted to the whole class one day how Cabbage is the only one in the class who always says, "You're welcome" all the time for everything. While it's great to hear that my child is polite outside of my watchful eyes, it saddens me to know that polite manners are the exception, not the norm.

For as many times as I have asked, "What do we say?" in hopes of hearing "Thank you", I can't stop asking it. My oldest child is twelve, so I have been asking that question for many years. Do they still sometimes forget to say thank you after dinner? Yes. Do I ever let a dinner go by where I don't ask, "What do you say for dinner?" No. I'm dedicated to the cause.

> *One morning, as Jane was deep in thought at her desk in the office, her bestie Sandy waltzed in and plopped down as she always did in the morning. "Ohmagosh, Jane!" she exclaimed. Not looking up immediately from her task, Jane calmly asked, "What's up, Sandy?" "What is so important that you can't pay attention to this conversation, Jane?!" Demanded Sandy with an increasingly irritated tone of voice.*

"How can I help you today, Sandy?" Jane looked up and mocked her friend with a sickeningly sweet tone. "Bitch, please," Sandy jested and then flipped the switch back to her enthusiastic storytelling voice, "So, we spent the weekend at my in-laws' house, and my mother-in-law pulled me aside to tell me that my kids weren't being very polite," she explained. "What do you mean, exactly?" Asked Jane, giving her friend her full attention and realizing her work would have to wait on Sandy.

"My mom cooked the whole weekend, and my kids never said 'thank you', I guess. She had the nerve to tell me that I needed to do better at teaching my kids some manners! Can you even believe that?!" She pointedly asked Jane.

"Well, Sandy, are you modeling the right behavior, and are you holding your children to a standard of good manners at home? I mean, I love you, but you're kind of a little abrasive sometimes." Jane confessed. "That's rude," Sandy retorted and then paused. "What are you saying?" she continued.

"I'm just saying that maybe you and Jason need to be better examples when it comes to modeling the behavior you want your kids to have; that's all," Jane said. *"Dick and I try really hard to be polite to each other while also making sure Joy is always minding her P's and Q's."* Sandy stewed in annoyance for a few moments and added, *"Yeah, but that will be hard to do. Jason has always been kind of rude; his parents are that way too. I don't see how I'm going to be able to change him in order to then change the boys. And... honestly, it hasn't been going that well in our marriage for a while anyway,"* Sandy confessed. *"But I will try my hardest to model better manners and try to remember to keep on my kids too,"* said her voice with the smallest hint of sadness.

How can you know if what you're doing at home is working with your kids? You'll know when they are outside of the home environment and not around you. When my boys spend a week at their Grandparents' house, or when they are with their father and run into one of my work friends who's out shopping, they are always polite. Why? Because I'm sure they hear my voice in their heads just like I hear my dad's voice in my head about my retirement or working smarter, not harder.

Yes, it's annoying to have to keep saying the same thing over and over and over and over again, but I promise that consistency pays off. I have heard, "They are the politest children I've ever met." "They're so well-behaved!" While sometimes I think that they aren't the best-behaved children, I do realize how great they are when I encounter children who are a little more monster than human.

Cabbage has recently emerged from his monster-stage chrysalis, and he has been magically transformed into a very helpful and subservient child. I'm not sure what changed him from a little terrorist to my minion, but I'll take it. One evening as I was relaxing on the couch, I asked him if he would get me my dessert from the refrigerator. "Don't get up Mommy, you're relaxing. I'll do it." he said as he rushed off to play butler. I watched him retrieve a napkin and wrap a fork in it, just like at a restaurant. He brought it over, both hands extended, presented it, and said, "Here you go, Mommy." Why was he being so nice? Was I dying and I was the last to know? Nope. Good parenting procedures were producing great results!

Hearing platitudes of gratitude is great when you have made dinner after a long day of work and playing kid shuttle service, but what's even better? Having your children put their dishes in the dishwasher and start it. Oh yes, we have arrived at the pinnacle of success! Anthony is the slowest eater on the planet. I think every family has one. It's painful.

The rule used to be that you cleared your dishes and put them by the sink when you were finished, and Andy (when he is here) or I will load and start the dishwasher. Andy finally decided not to finish doing the dishes until the last person, Anthony, was done because progress always halted until then anyway.

Shortly after Andy's pattern changed, I taught the boys how to load the dishwasher because if someone is too slow and misses the first round of dish clearing and loading, then that person is on his own... Anthony! Teaching Cabbage to load the dishwasher was easy because he's the one who unloads the dishwasher. We are still working on reminding them to load and start the dishwasher, but that's because the change is still relatively fresh. It is wonderful, though, seeing them grow, change, and easily accept more responsibility.

Beyond the kitchen and words of sincerity, there are acts of chivalry and etiquette that I am determined to have my boys master. There are a few ways in which door holding open can and should be taught. The first is through repetition and consistency. My boys learned years ago to hold the door open when we go into the school in the morning. I keep my hands in my pockets and say, "Would you get the door, please?" They often carry backpacks and an extra bag of snow gear, but they are still happy to do it. Seeing my husband consistently opening every door for me also drives home the lesson I am trying to teach.

Behavior modeling has such a strong effect on behavior because not only do they hear what needs to be done, they learn by seeing it done.

Cabbage goes to the after-school program in the afternoons because a mom can only tolerate sitting in one parent pickup nightmare in a day. One day, when I arrived, Cabbage ran up to the door, and I asked him, "Do you want me to go inside and sign you out, or do you want to do it?" "I'll do it, Mommy. You look comfortable," he said sweetly and ran off.

As I pulled ahead and watched my son approach the doors to the school, I saw him stop and for a second, I wondered what he was doing. A moment later, I saw him open the door and stand on the other side to hold it open for a mom and her two little girls. In that proud moment, I knew what I had been teaching every day had sunk in.

When you have made it miles down the road of teaching manners and being polite, you enter into the ask-and-you-shall-receive phase. I used to dread my weekends when my littles were little. People would ask me, "What are your plans for the weekend?" and my canned, sarcastic response always was, "Try to survive." There is a point at which children are just so much work, especially for a single working mom.

Finally, over my weekend PTSD, I can now ask them to help, and they will. I used to get frazzled on the weekends in the winter when they come in for lunch. They used to leave a pile of wet, dirty winter gear at the back door, which I had to deal with while making their lunch. Now, however, when they come in, they put their wet snow pants and jackets in the dryer with two dryer sheets to minimize the warm, dirty boy smell, and they put their wet gloves on the glove dryer and turn it on. With progressive responsibility teaching, my boys now make their lunches and clean up after themselves too, and mommy no longer fears her weekends. I find myself smiling at the progress we have made as a family.

HER KIDS SAID

Mom: Do you think that it is important to say please and thank you?

Both: Yes!

Mom: Why?

Anthony: Because it's good manners.

Cabbage: It's polite.

Mom: How do you think you would feel if you went to all the work of planning, paying for, and making dinner, and no one said, "Thank You"?

Cabbage: (*Releases the cat back to freedom*) Disrespect.

Mom: You would feel disrespected?

Both: Yeah.

Mom: That's it?

Anthony: Because you're not doing anything about it, so…

Mom: Well, if you did all of that, and no one said, "Thank you", you'd just be like…

Anthony: That would be rude. Obviously.

Mom: Do you think it's important to hold the door open for others?

Both: Yes!

Mom: Why?

Anthony: Especially women. Because, uh, it's a way to show… You care?

Mom: Cabbage?

Cabbage: I don't know why. I just do it because it's nice.

Mom: Who should you hold the door open for?

Cabbage: Everyone!

Anthony: Well, most people, yes.

Cabbage: Unless someone is rude… then they don't, yeah.

Mom: How does being able to do more things to help Mommy, like putting your wet snow gear in the dryer or vacuuming, make you feel?

Both: Good!

Mom: Why do you help most times without saying no or being sassy?

Cabbage: Because I love you, Mommy.

Anthony: You're a good mom (*gives me a thumbs up*)

Mom: Awe. So sweet!

It's never too late to instill good manners and etiquette in your children; however, the later you start, the harder training will be. If you can start modeling good behavior before you have children, you're miles ahead in the "Please and Thank You" game.

The caveat to being successful in teaching these pleasantries is the same as most parenting goals… you need not suck at the goal if you expect your children not to suck at it, either. Just keep your expectations in check. If your child is as polite as you and your partner are or aren't, that's the best you can hope for, fortunately, or unfortunately.

If you have politeness goals for your children that exceed your current behavior, then the whole family will need to come together and find a way to get on Team Suck Less at Manners because it's either all or nothing when it comes to system changes in the home.

Chapter 16:

Video Games are the Fast Food of Play Time

M.O.M. SAID

While technological advances are making our lives easier, they also encourage a more sedentary lifestyle. That lifestyle, combined with the convenience of unhealthy food options, is leading to the fact that roughly two out of every three American adults are overweight or obese. These odds are not a good foreshadowing of the future health and longevity of our children. It's so easy to choose unhealthy foods because most of the time, they taste better, are cheaper, and are more convenient to make than cooking meals from scratch. And we all know how much easier it is to shove a device in a kid's face than it is to go outside and play with them when we're busy.

As a person who tries very hard to live a healthy lifestyle, I am constantly trying to reiterate to my children how to make smart decisions about food and activity. However, I find it challenging to make homemade dinners on school nights or have a civilized meal without their iPads to keep them from embarrassing me at restaurants. Do I sometimes allow iPads at dinner or choose the blue box with the yellow noodles on it for dinner? Yes, but I try to make that blue box dinner with broccoli if I need to resort to those measures.

My bestie told me once that the yellow dye in the original blue box would cause colon cancer, so I tried switching to a different, healthier brand. The kids hated it. "What is this? This isn't mac and cheese!" they protested. "Well, my friend said that the other stuff would give you colon cancer," I explained. "What's a colon?" They asked. "It's part of your butt," I oversimplified. "The other stuff will give us butt cancer?" They asked as they burst out laughing.

When it comes to food as it pertains to teaching healthy living, there are several different areas of focus: meals, snacks, and candy/sugar. When it comes to meal planning, I try to make as many meals from scratch as time allows, and I try to incorporate as many fruits and vegetables as I can: all-fruit smoothies with burgers, parmesan chicken with broccoli, bananas with lunch, and a fruit or veggie side is a must if the meal leans more toward the unhealthy.

Snacks sent to school are veggie chips and fruit strips or fruit squeeze pouches and kids' protein bars. Snacks at home are usually fresh grapes, which my children are split on: Anthony prefers red grapes, and Cabbage prefers green. Go figure. Special food requests are not something I usually support, but when it comes to fruit, I'll gladly make exceptions. I want my children to grow up and choose the fruits they like over other unhealthy options. Cabbage is partial to his grapes being frozen in the summer. The cotton candy-flavored ones make a great snack on the beach that also helps keep the rest of the food chilled!

Sugar is a sticky situation, but I found a way to use an unfortunate event to my advantage, "If you eat too much sugar, you'll get diarrhea. Do you want to get diarrhea? Do you remember that time when you got it and how bad it was?" I ask my boys. I'm not sure what caused the upset stomach issue that one time, way back when, but I took that opportunity to blame it on the amount of sugar consumed, and I've been pulling it out whenever necessary ever since. Anthony will dump out ice cream or put back M&M's sometimes for fear of revenge from the gastrointestinal gods.

Food choices aren't the only factor when it comes to encouraging a healthy lifestyle. There's this thing called exercise that most people do not get enough of. Back in my day... we used to play outside. We didn't have iPads or video games, and we didn't even have internet. I know I sound like a cliché old person, but I'm getting up there. In all seriousness, kids spend too much time on their devices or staring at a screen, and it's a systemic issue. Parenting has never had such an easy crutch to fall on than shoving an iPad into a child's face, and they do it because it works.

I'm guilty of it too, but I have screen time hours of operation and kick the kids outside whenever possible. In the winter, I incentivize with, "If you stay out for at least thirty minutes, you can have hot chocolate with marshmallows at lunch," I promise as I start the clock. "How much time have we been outside?" They question as one of them pokes a frozen face inside the door. If they last longer than thirty minutes, they usually get extra mini marshmallows on the side or in the hot cocoa.

In Duluth, Minnesota we have a saying: "There's no such thing as bad weather, just bad clothing." We earn the right to say that because we all go outside in all types of weather to get to work or school. That's what hand warmers, boot warmers, and outerwear rated to negative fifty are for. Of course, I make exceptions for lightning and inclement weather... I'm not a complete psycho... unless I don't get enough sleep.

> *Joy had been begging to have her friend Poppy over for a Saturday play date. Poppy had gotten a new virtual reality set for her birthday, and Joy had already been over to Poppy's house once to play with it.*

"I don't want to encourage more screen time," explained Jane. "I like Poppy. I think she's a good friend, and I want you to be able to have her over to play, but you will need to play outside together. No video games." she forewarned. Pouting, Joy reluctantly agreed, knowing full well that fighting with her mother was futile. She never won, so she took what she could get.

Jane texted Poppy's mom, "Does Poppy want to come over this Saturday to play with Joy? If so, please send appropriate outdoor boots, hats, and mittens because they are going to play outside." Poppy's mom texted back, "I would love that! Sounds like a great plan. I have been trying to get Poppy away from that virtual reality set, and it hasn't been easy."

The easiest way to get your kiddos outside is to go outside with them. That means you must participate too, but we can all use more exercise in our lives. I find that even if only one of the adults is outside, and even if that adult is mowing and not playing with the kids, children will still go outside with less prompting than if they aren't alone outside. If you only have one child, I suggest trying to partner up with a neighbor with a child around the same age because two are always better than one when it comes to outdoor playtime.

What I find ironic about the evolution of video games is that virtual reality was invented to be an experience of going somewhere and doing something different. How about this novel idea: go outside and do something different? Playing outside and using your imagination is the original VR, and it's better for your brain, your heart, your muscles, and your social skills. No VR can be better than a child's imagination. Imagination is free and needs to be tapped into and encouraged.

I don't recall my parents entertaining my sister and me. They were busy running a business. My sister and I were outside all the time doing who knows what. I remember days that I would spend hours crouched over a patch of clover, looking for the anomalies with four leaves. I found quite a few, pressed them, and preserved them between two pieces of clear packaging tape.

Can you imagine proposing hours of four-leaf clover hunting to a child today? I can. I tried. I think it lasted for thirty seconds. Even though they had no interest in finding lucky clovers, I am proud of my boys for their ingenuity outside. One summer afternoon, I walked outside to see a camouflage wall made from ferns and a chain link fence. Their hands were stained green, their clothing was filthy, and they smelled awful, but they were learning teamwork and creativity.

Sometimes, I see them outside with my old pots and pans, playing cooking games or protecting the yard with walkie-talkies. On rainy days, they will work on a box fort in the basement or invent games that require running laps around my kitchen island while avoiding the strangest obstacles.

The best toys that encouraged my boys to go outside were plastic training axes that they used to chop down a dead tree, wood whittling knives that they used to create swords from sticks, and imaginations fostered by being forced to go outside and be creative. Having chosen a second husband who is very much into weapons, it only stands to reason that he would build a weapon-throwing wall in the yard. What did he buy the boys for Christmas? Throwing stars, of course. That's one way to get kids outside... let them throw sharp, metal objects.

Despite my hesitation to let the boys play with them, throwing them responsibly is quite fun. The whole family participates in weapon throwing, which has evolved into a collection of throwing knives, throwing stars, and throwing axes. "Ninja training" is what Andy calls it. Sharp object throwing combined with the obstacle course strung between the trees does resemble ninja training.

> *Jane had just passed her 40th birthday, and she was starting to feel her metabolism slow down, almost as if it was happening minute by minute, hour by hour. Being able to eat whatever she wanted without a dedicated exercise routine was starting to catch up with her, and her clothes weren't fitting. The weight gain was starting to make her feel down about herself.*

Dick noticed this change in his wife, but he was hesitant to say anything, the smart man that he was. To his surprise, one morning, Jane said to him, "I need to change something because I feel like I'm gaining weight at an exponential rate, and I don't like how I look or feel anymore."

"What are you thinking?" Ask Dick, careful not to offer any unsolicited weight-loss advice. "Well, I think I might want to exercise at home on a treadmill..." "I'll support you and whatever you want to do, dear. We can go look at treadmills this weekend if you'd like." Dick encouraged.

Not only had Jane been gaining some extra weight, but Joy had also become a little more sedentary in her free time as well. She had found a video game on her phone that she could not seem to get enough of.

Jane was ready to go as soon as the new treadmill arrived. She was committed to making a change and got right on it. A week into her new routine of morning exercise, she started to feel better. Noticing that her mother had made a significant lifestyle change and how it seemed to make her happier, Joy asked if she could try running on the treadmill as well.

"Sure honey, just make sure that you are safe when you're there and pay attention. Don't start too fast." she instructed.

Sure enough, as the weeks and months went by, both Jane and Joy were enjoying the benefits of regular exercise, and when the seasons changed and it warmed up outside, they decided to go running together. Now instead of spending time together on the couch, they spent it doing something healthy and fun.

Exercise is one of the hardest things to incorporate into your daily routine if you haven't found the internal motivation or if you never had that behavior modeled for you by a caregiver. My husband and I are daily exercisers, and my kids see us doing it and take it as normal adult behavior. When it's nice outside, I like to take the boys for a walk and get what I call "bonus exercise."

If you're not a frequent exerciser, it's never too late to start. If you're trying to start while teaching your children the lesson you are learning, do it together. If you exercise as a family, you can take that time to multitask some fireside chats. Just try not to get lost on a hike like we did once. We all got bonus exercise that day as we traipsed through the woods, hoping not to become "meat for the animals" as Cabbage so elegantly put it.

HER KIDS SAID

Mom: How much sugar and candy do you think is a smart choice to eat in a day?

Cabbage: (*Annoyed, and throws his hands up*) Well, how am I supposed to know that about sugar and candy!?

Mom: How much do you think in your brain now?

Cabbage: Not a lot, that's for sure.

Anthony: A lot! (*Laughs*)

Mom: Do you think it's healthy?

Cabbage: Even one piece isn't! Even like…

Anthony: Any candy isn't healthy.

Mom: When you're at school, do you choose white or chocolate milk, and why?

Cabbage: None.

Mom: You don't choose any milk?

Cabbage: I pick the milk, but I don't drink it. I pick chocolate, even though I don't drink it.

Anthony: I pick chocolate, and I drink it all the time.

Mom: Is there a reason that you decided to choose chocolate even though I told you not to?

Anthony: Because the white one tastes like garbage, and the chocolate one tastes like cold chocolate instead of hot chocolate.

Cabbage: It's actually true! It tastes SO bad!

Anthony: White tastes like the carton itself.

Cabbage: (*Making snoring noises*)

Mom: How important do you think daily exercise is?

Both: Very important!

Mom: Why?

Anthony: Otherwise, then you wouldn't be healthy.

Cabbage: Otherwise, you're gonna get (*gestures a big belly*) POOH – Fat!

Anthony: And you wouldn't be healthy at all, and you wouldn't...

Cabbage: Yeah.

Mom: What kind of exercise do you think you will do when you are a grown-up?

Cabbage: Doin' what you do. Go downstairs on the treadmill.

Anthony: Yeah, but what if you don't have a treadmill?

Mom: Anthony?

Anthony: Running, but not just plain old running. Running downhill, running uphill...

Mom: What do you think it means to live a healthy lifestyle?

Cabbage: Um, you don't eat like, too much candy or like junk food. You mostly wanna exercise or eat fruits or vegetables.

Anthony: And try not to sit like a couch potato. Or sit on the phone and do nothing all day, every day.

Mom: What things do we do as a family that are healthy?

Anthony: Eat healthy food.

Cabbage: Eat a ton of fruit and vegetables, we always play outside a ton, or so something in the house, or go downstairs and…

Mom: As a family, though, together.

Anthony: Oh, we exercise and run.

Mom: Like, we go for walks together in the summer. What things do you think we can improve on to be healthier?

Cabbage: Don't eat too much candy! I got one! I already said it, though. Don't eat too much candy, and don't play too much iPad or video games.

Mom: That's right. Turn around, Anthony. Would you rather go for a walk with Mom or play Minecraft together?

Both: Go on a walk.

Mom: What is your favorite thing to do outside?

Cabbage: That's a hard one.

Anthony: Would that include swimming?

Mom: Yeah.

Cabbage: No, going to the water park.

Mom: Well, I meant like an activity like biking, or what games you play in the yard... more like localized outside here.

Anthony: Like playing outside, doing random stuff like biking.

Cabbage: Just make up games and have fun.

Mom: What is your favorite season to play outside in, and why?

Cabbage: Winter!

Anthony: Suuummmmeeeerrrr.

Mom: Why winter?

Cabbage: Because you can build stuff like a fort, have a snowball fight, build a castle, and you can build battles. You can do anything in Minecraft or any video game and make it true. Like you could do a zombie apocalypse – you just gotta make these snowmen and then you get snowballs, and you go like (*makes rapid-fire gun sounds and motions*), and then they're dead.

Mom: Anthony, why do you like summer for outside?

Anthony: Because it's way easier to move around, and you can do a lot more water stuff, and walking, and playing and fun with your friends instead of having to put on a thousand layers just to play outside, and you can't even move around.

Mom: What is your favorite family outdoor activity?

Cabbage: How'm I supposed to know?

Anthony: Walking!

Mom: (*Whispering the answer*) Going to the beach...

Both: (*Faces light up*) Going to the beach!

Mom: Yeah. Why do you like to go outside when there's an adult outside, even if that adult isn't playing with you?

Cabbage: Because I feel more safe, and if I need help or something, they're right there, and I can just ask.

Anthony: It's just better because then you don't make dumb mistakes outside.

Cabbage: Like fall on your face…

Mom: Are you afraid that you're going to make dumb mistakes outside?

Anthony: Sometimes, like going too far back (*beyond the property line*)… cuz I like doing that, like running away from home. That'd be fun.

Mom: Okay. That's a weird answer.

With greater and more interesting technological advances comes greater parental responsibility to resist relying on it to do our parenting for us. iPads and video games have become the fast food of playtime. An easy but unhealthy option.

Healthy living is a hard lifestyle to adopt if you haven't found a way to do so already. If it was easy, everyone would do it, but it's not easy, and sometimes it just sucks. There are many days when I wake up and say, "I wish I didn't need to exercise. It would be so much easier if I didn't care." And then I get up and exercise because I know that if I don't, I'll feel sluggish all day and eat more too.

Times and technology have changed our world, but one fact will always remain the same: kids need to be allowed time to be kids, and they should be outside being creative and expending energy as much as possible. That kid boredom that we all dread is when patience and persistence can pay off. Patience in waiting for them to invent some new game and persistence in sticking to your word that it's a no-technology time of the day.

If you find yourself wanting to make a change for the healthier for your family, start small: exchange an unhealthy side for a fruit or veggie, substitute fruit for a snack, and take short walks with your whole family. Make those walks a game by looking for specific items on the walk or guessing the real estate costs of houses you pass (I play guess-the-house-price sometimes with my boys because I can multitask money conversations along with teaching healthy living).

Get creative and try new things as a family. It will take time, but if you can find the motivation to start and keep it going, it will benefit you and your health and could positively impact the health of your family and subsequent generations.

Chapter 17:

Parenting Through The Big D – Divorce

M.O.M. SAID

The D-word. The thing no one ever thinks will happen to them as they walk down the aisle full of love, hope, and sometimes naiveté. Well, it does happen despite the best of efforts. While divorce is never a fun, easy, or trauma-less life-changing event, when there are children involved, the fallout can be much more devastating.

When my first marriage was ending after fourteen years, we had a four-year-old and a seven-year-old. I wrestled with the thought of divorce because of the effect it could have on my children. Children of divorce always seemed to have some residual issues tied to the trauma, and

I was already scared to screw up my kids without a divorce, making it more inevitable.

I remember when my ex and I went to our first court appearance to dissolve the marriage. Neither of us had lawyers, we had filed the petition together, and the judge said, "I want to commend you for having an amicable divorce. I wish more people would be this agreeable for the sake of the children like you are."

And that's it. That's the key to helping your children through a divorce. Never talk negatively about your ex in front of them, never try to be the more fun or generous parent in hopes of making the other parent look bad, never let them hear you talking about the nitty gritty of the divorce, and never ever let them hear you fighting. As much as you can keep the behind-the-scenes of the divorce behind the scenes, the better.

After all, it's not their fault things didn't work out, but they are the ones who will need to adapt and be shuttled back and forth. When we divorced, we tried to stay on the same page about our parenting styles as much as possible. For the most part, we had always agreed on discipline, consistency, etc. Consistency between households helped greatly during the transition. Just because you are no longer together does not mean you aren't on the same parenting team.

We let the school and summer care program know that our family was going through a divorce and to let us know if they saw any signs that we needed to intervene. I think there was only one instance of a behavior note that got sent home, but that was it. Grades were good, attitudes were good, and it was the best-case scenario because we kept it away from them and weren't vindictive.

If your custody schedule isn't 50/50, it's helpful to make your children calendars that show where they will be and when. I made them calendars with pictures and colors illustrating Mom's House, Dad's House, No School, Grandma's House, Spring Break, etc. They used those calendars for years, crossing off the days so they felt like they had security in knowing where they would be. Yes, it was a lot of work, but I would do it all over again to help them feel safe in the transition.

> Jane's work friend Sandy had become increasingly distracted and agitated at work, so Jane decided to find out what was up. Closing Sandy's office door behind her, Jane probed, "Sandy, you seem really off lately. Are you okay?" As Sandy's nose reddened and her eyes moistened, Jane braced herself for something big.
>
> "Jason asked for a divorce." she burst out as she began to ugly cry. "Oh, I'm so sorry Sandy," Jane offered as she got up to hug her friend. "I mean, I kind of saw it coming," confessed Sandy, "But what am I going to tell my kids? How will they handle it? I just don't know what to do." she cried.
>
> "Have you had a chance to talk with Jason about how you both can proceed in a way that is the least harmful to the children?" Jane asked. "He said I can have the house, and that he wants what's best for the kids, I don't know. He said that all he wants is a chance to start over."
>
> "Well, that's kind of rude!" Jane empathized. "But at least he's willing to try to work with you to make

the situation not horrible for the kids." Jane reasoned. "Yeah," Sandy sniffled through a plugged-up nose. "At least we have that in common still. Wanting to keep the kids as sheltered from our drama as much as possible."

One of the challenges in splitting up the adults is that if one of the parents used to handle all of the school things or logistics and the other didn't, there can be a disruption that affects the children if field trip fees or lunches don't get sent, or pajama day is forgotten. In instances like that when you don't feel like you should have to parent your ex-spouse, you should still do your best to make sure the kids don't feel like they slipped through the cracks. I didn't and don't enjoy having to send little reminders to my ex, but I know he appreciates it, and I feel better knowing the kids aren't missing out on anything at school.

In the case of my first marriage, I was always the planner, so I have taken it upon myself to create a year-at-a-glance custody calendar so we each get our percentage of time and agreed-upon holidays. I send it to him for approval and once approved, I send Google calendar invites for the whole year, so we are always on the same page. I also send invites for No School days, regardless of whose turn it is to have the kids. Those reminders reduce the other reminders that may or may not need to be sent leading up to the day.

When it comes to one parent or the other needing to make a change to the schedule, try to be accommodating because you may need accommodating too. My ex travels a lot for work, and sometimes he asks me to pick up packages at his house. Sometimes I have things come up and need him to watch the kids. We make it happen, and we don't fight about it. Why? What good would that do anyone? Neither of us has family in town, so we have learned to rely on each other. He even came to my house to drive me to the hospital when I had a MRSA infection in my knee, and I offered to help with the kids or whatever he needed when his autoimmune disorder came back.

You do it for the kids. You treat each other with respect because you want to lead by example and because you want the very best for them regardless of the decisions you make. While you aren't in love with your former spouse anymore, that doesn't mean that you still don't care about their well-being.

Over five years after my divorce, the boys are starting to notice differences in the households and have formed their own opinions. It's like those photos where you have two almost identical pictures side-by-side and see little differences between them. While my ex and I still agree on most things, we have different bedtimes for the kids and different thoughts about dinner, snacks, and soda. The main thing is that we both emphasize the importance of good grades, not paying for grades, playing outside, respecting their parents, and being responsible.

No rule says that divorce has to be messy, expensive, or last for years. There is just no reason for it to be that way beyond pure spite and selfishness. If you find yourself in the unfortunate circumstance of a divorce with children, please pause and think about how to proceed in the best interest of your children.

No matter how you slice it, divorce is like death. It is the death of the family unit as you knew it. You go through a lot of the phases of grief on your way to accepting and moving on. Communicating with your children about why it is happening and that it isn't their fault is also essential to helping them make the transition.

HER KIDS SAID

Mom: Do you remember when Daddy and I told you that we were getting a divorce?

Anthony: What?

Mom: Do you remember when Daddy and I told you that we were getting a divorce?

Cabbage: I don't remember that, but I remember when you guys were arguing. Anthony was playing on his iPad upstairs, and you guys were arguing in the kitchen.

Mom: Thinking back to the time we were getting a divorce, how did you feel? Do you remember that? The transition?

Anthony: Not really, but it was kind of annoying and…

Mom: It was annoying, why?

Cabbage: I didn't know if I was sad, or mad, or happy.

Mom: You don't remember?

Cabbage: I remember kinds of being happy, or something like that.

Mom: Really?!

Cabbage: I don't know.

Mom: You don't have any feelings about it from back then?

Anthony: I don't remember.

Cabbage: I don't either.

Mom: So, it wasn't traumatizing to you then?

Anthony: Not really.

Mom: Okay, what was the hardest part about the divorce?

Anthony: You leaving.

Cabbage: You leaving. We couldn't see you for three or four weeks… or something like that.

Anthony: (*Voice gets quiet*) yeah.

Mom: Is there anything that you can think of that made the transition easier for you?

Cabbage: Um, like what do you mean?

Mom: Like I kinda think that it made it easier for you when I made you those calendars so you knew where you would be.

Anthony: Yeah.

Cabbage: Yeah.

Mom: Is there anything that when you look back, you can say, "I'm glad I had this because it helped me transition back and forth"?

Cabbage: The calendars you made.

Anthony: I just knew sometimes because you guys had the same pattern.

Mom: We had the same rules?

Anthony: Yeah.

Mom: Looking back, how do you feel about the divorce now at this point? Five years later.

Anthony: I really don't care, kinda. I don't hardly remember at all.

Cabbage: Kinda happy it happened.

Mom: Why? Because now I'm happier.

Both: Yeah.

Cabbage: And because now we have Andy and the cat!

Mom: If you could give one piece of advice to parents with children getting divorced, what would it be?

Cabbage: Hmmm, that's a tough one. Like for the parents or for the kids? (*distracted by the cat lying across both of their laps*)

Mom: Both.

Cabbage: The kids should help both parents out so when they do it, they get rewarded. And plus, that means that they would like both houses because they would get rewarded. I don't know if that'd be good, but I just thought of it.

Anthony: I can't really think of anything.

Mom: No advice for parents to help make that transition?

Cabbage: The parents should do um, like nice things for the kids because they just got divorced. They would like, um, let's see. Do what they ask.

Like if the kid said, "Can you ask my friend if we can have a sleepover?"

Mom: So, you think that parents should give extra nice things when they get divorced to the children and not just stick to the normal guidelines and rules?

Cabbage: Well, stick to the normal rules because it would be pretty expensive if they did that.

Mom: If they changed the rules, then that would actually be worse because isn't it better to stay consistent?

Cabbage: Yeah, stay consistent. I don't really know.

I think that the last round of comprehensive questioning may have been a little above their pay grade, but Kudos to them for giving it a shot. Divorce with children involved is something that should be handled with as much emotional maturity as both parents can muster. While they may harbor extremely poignant feelings toward their former partner, both parents need to practice what they preach and stop their bad behavior before it starts.

If making the transition easier for your children means lying on the altar of sacrifice to help your new ex, then do it! If he needs reminding of something they need for school, or that it's pajama day, or that it's parent-teacher conferences suck it up and continue to work together as a team when it pertains to any matter involving the children. No, you're not married anymore, and it's not your job to babysit your ex anymore, but it will always be your job to look out for the welfare of your children.

The more you can shelter your children from the mess of a divorce, the easier the transition will be and the less it will have a negative effect on them. If you find yourself in this unfortunate situation, try your very hardest to suck less at traumatizing your children with the issues you and your partner have with each other.

Chapter 18:

The Delicate Dance of the Stepchildren

M.O.M. SAID

When I hear the word "stepmother", I envision the evil stepmother from the original animated Cinderella movie. Never in my wildest dreams did I envision that title one day being my own. Not the evil part... just the stepmother part.

With the rising rate of marital failures, blended families are becoming more common. Parenting becomes a very delicate dance when stepchildren enter the picture. Sometimes it's your kids with your new partner, sometimes it's your partner's child or children and you, and sometimes it's both. Regardless of the ingredients of your blended family recipe, the result isn't usually as Brady Bunch as we would like it to be.

The delicate dance of stepchildren reminds me of the children's song and dance "Ring Around the Rosie". *"Ring-a-Ring-a-Roses is all about the Great Plague, the apparent whimsy being a foil for one of London's most atavistic dreads (thanks to the Black Death). The fatalism of the rhyme is brutal: the roses are a euphemism for deadly rashes, the posies a supposed preventative measure; the a-tishoos pertain to sneezing symptoms, and the implication of everyone falling down is, well, death."* (Library of Congress Blog, 2014). Okay, it's not THAT bad, but dancing the dance of stepchildren is a minefield.

The first issue you will run into if you have children from a previous relationship is the timing of introducing them to your new partner. It's a tough call because, in an ideal situation, you would be certain of the longevity of the relationship AND your ex would be on board with the introduction of another adult figure in your children's lives. Unfortunately, the ideal situation hardly ever happens.

In many instances, the person who was asked for a divorce is more combative and unsupportive of any new person entering their children's lives.

My friend who is actively dating has met some men whose timeline of introducing their children to her seemed like a red flag. I think I'm safe in assuming that if someone wants to introduce you to his child on date number two, that's a big parenting red flag.

During my short trip to Single Town, I went on a few dates with a local guy. While he seemed great on paper, I saw a few red flags when I peppered him with my twenty questions. When I asked why he hadn't had any children, he responded, "I never really thought about it." That answer erased him from the option of ever meeting my kids. In over forty years of life, he never thought about having kids. That's weird. In my mind, if he'd never thought about it, I didn't think he should make the stepdad shortlist. I don't do anything inefficiently, especially date. The local guy was nice to hang out with, but he was never going to be my second husband.

The sting of Sandy's divorce had lessened over the six months after it was finalized. She decided not to stay in the house with all the memories, so she found a new little place where she could start over, and her life was finally starting to find a new rhythm. "I'm so proud of you, Sandy!" applauded Jane as they spent the afternoon painting the living room of Sandy's new home.

"Do you think it's too soon to start dating again?" Sandy asked with sheepish trepidation. "No, I don't think it's ever too soon if you feel like you've healed and are healthy enough to move on," Jane encouraged. "Good!" replied Sandy, "Because I've met someone, and I reeealllllllyy like him." Trying to hide her shock, Jane replied, "Where did you meet him, and what's his name?"

"His name is Alan, and I met him in our office," she grinned at Jane. "How did I not catch this?!" Shrieked Jane. "I know I've been really busy with that big project, but… when did this start?" she pushed. "Oh, about a month ago… He approached me one day when he brought me an email I had left on the printer. He was so awkward, it was cute. He mumbled something about maybe grabbing some lunch after the training we were going to be in, and I agreed. I never really noticed him before, but he doesn't usually come up to our floor," she said as the flush of new romance colored her cheeks.

"Back up, lady," Jane interjected. "I need more details." "Well, he has two girls. One is 18, and the other is 23." she elaborated. "Uh oh, you know what JoJo always says about men with daughters..." warned Jane. "Yeah, stay away from them! But he's so nice to me, and he's kind of handsome in that nerdy Clark Kent kind of a way."

"Have you given any thought to how you will introduce your little boys to him and vice versa?" asked Jane. "No, not yet. I think it's too early, but I guess I should probably decide on some sort of plan just in case it heads in that direction," she agreed.

When I met my second husband after my divorce, I knew within the first month that he was going to be in my life for a very long time, and I decided that I was going to introduce him to my boys. If they weren't going to mesh well, I would have to give him up, and I wanted to get on with it. I know a month seems too soon, but it felt right. I would never have introduced him to my children if I hadn't seen the real possibility of a successful long-term relationship.

Did I speak to my ex-husband about introducing the children to Andy beforehand? Yes. They're his kids too. He thought it too early and wasn't overly supportive, but to be fair, he hadn't asked for the divorce, which was still a fresh, unhealed wound. Andy's mom also had her reservations, "Oh Andy, again with the kids?" she knew how attached he became to children in his past relationships and how heartbroken he was after losing the connection to the children of his former partners.

That first weekend when the man I knew would be my second husband met my little loves is something I'll never forget. Anthony was very tentative, standoffish, and a little quiet, while his little brother Cabbage, who was four, jumped right into playing army guys with Andy. It's a strange thing to watch, like when you introduce a new pet to an existing pet. What was going to happen? The next morning, they flanked him at the table as they ate breakfast, excited to find out more about him. There's a photo I have of the three of them, and Anthony is pulling up Andy's sleeve to look at his tattoos. "Are these permanent?" he asked. "Yes," Andy answered. "Like will they be there forever?" "Yes." Adorable.

When children are introduced to a new partner, the connection cannot be rushed. The kids took to Andy quickly because of his easy-going nature, childlike demeanor, and willingness to play with them. Now five and a half years later, the moment they step foot back into my house after time with Dad, the first thing they ask me is, "Is Andy here?" or "When is Andy coming back?" Not, "Hi, Mommy. We missed you!" I don't think that they could have bonded any better than they have.

After you've successfully made introductions of your children to your new partner, the next hurdle to jump over is parenting styles and finding out if they align. Parenting style misalignment is an extremely sticky situation to navigate. What rules are hard and fast, who disciplines and how, schedule adherence, food preferences, approved or unapproved screen time, etc. Either party that enters this situation with children in tow brings with them their personal parenting preferences. But what happens when you and your new partner aren't on the same page?

I'll tell you what happens. You stupidly assume that they will parent as you do, and they likely assume the same. Sometimes, you naively expect them to parent your kids like you do when you aren't around. This clashing of parenting styles has plagued my relationship, and it's still something that I'm actively trying very hard to suck less at managing.

> *Six months into her relationship with Alan, Sandy had a discussion with him about bringing the families together to meet. "I think it would make life a lot easier if we let our kids in on our relationship, don't you?" Sandy asked Alan. "Yeah, my daughters know about you, and they've been asking questions, but I didn't want to rush you." he agreed. "Great, let's plan a casual introduction... how about we have a picnic at our favorite spot?" she suggested. "Neutral territory and a place for the kids to bond; I like it," he agreed.*

As both families approached the meeting spot, Sandy's kids bolted toward Alan, who had brought frisbees and balls for the kids. "Hey guys, I thought maybe we could play together today. What do you think?" "Yeah!" her boys shouted together as they took a ball and ran off. "Girls, I'd like you to meet Sandy." Said Alan as he watched the women in his life make contact for the first time.

"Alan, Alan! Come play with us!" Sandy's boys begged while transferring dirt onto him as they tugged at his hands. "Okay, let's go!" he said as he took off ahead of them. Sandy smiled at how well they were getting along, but then she turned back to his daughters, who were now farther away and both on their phones. "Hey girls, what are you playing?" Sandy tried. They both uttered something she couldn't hear and wandered off. "This isn't going to be as easy as I'd hoped," she thought to herself.

My parenting style involves to-the-minute scheduling and immediate correction for disobeying rules... I run a tight ship. Despite his history of being in the military, Andy functions better under command than in command when it comes to parenting. Before I realized what needed to be done to correct the parenting misalignment in our relationship, I would get annoyed at him when I would ask him to "go tell the kids to stop (insert bad behavior here)." They wouldn't listen to him, and he would come back and tell me that they wouldn't listen.

I was annoyed that I had to go do the task I asked him to do because it was stupid and inefficient to do something twice. It didn't take long to realize that a solution needed to be presented so that we could both be on the same page and not on opposite teams. One day, I asked him, "What role would you like to have with my children? Would you like to have a co-disciplinarian role, or would you like to be 'fun uncle'?" "I'd rather be 'fun uncle'," he explained, "because they have a father."

As much as I wanted him to answer the way I wanted him to answer, I had to respect his decision and adjust my expectations. "Okay, I will take on the role of disciplinarian, and I will try not to ask you to do it or get mad at you for not doing it." After that boundary was established, I have tried to respect his decision. When he is at my house, I don't ask him to discipline my kids, and when I leave him in charge, I just know that I will come home to a mess and perhaps some of my rules having been disobeyed. It's the concession I've had to make, knowing full well that I cannot and should not try to change him.

When you and your significant other do not have the same parenting style, co-parenting is extremely difficult because of the lack of consistency, which is vital to the success of any child's well-being. When that misalignment happens, if you can adjust your and your children's expectations of the new person's role, you can still maintain consistency. Everyone just needs to get the same memo with the job descriptions of every authority figure.

On the other side of stepparenting is becoming the stepparent. In my case, Andy's daughter was eighteen when we met. I was unsure of what my place was with her; she had a mother, and I was a mother to other children. Was I supposed to try to befriend her, was I supposed to mentor her?

Where to step next so I didn't step on a landmine…

Andy's mom advised, "She'll come to you when she's ready." Okay, I was cordial but not pushy. Since my parents never split, I had no idea what she had been through in the fifteen years between when her parents divorced and her then eighteenth year of life. How had her father's many relationships affected her, and how would she feel about me, given how those other women had treated her? The path ahead looked like a dangerous minefield that I would need to navigate with caution.

> *Sandy didn't have much contact with Alan's girls after the picnic. They were adults, but they both still lived with Dad. "When do you think that your girls might move out?" Sandy asked as she stepped carefully onto the minefield of potential stepparenting." "I don't know," Alan said with a very cavalier attitude. "Do you think that maybe they should be preparing to move out and live on their own?" Sandy asked as her foot hovered over a hidden mine.*

"Why does this matter to you?!" Snapped Alan. Sandy could practically feel the shockwave as she stepped on the mine, and it exploded in her face. "I didn't mean to upset you," she retorted, "I just thought that if we were going to move in together, maybe it would make sense to start helping them get on their own feet." "I don't want to talk about this right now," huffed Alan. "They know that they need to move out at some point, and I trust them to take the necessary steps to do that."

"But do they know what those steps are? I mean, I was already married and had a full-time career at the age of 23. I feel like you may be doing your girls a disservice by handling them with kid gloves and not allowing them the opportunity to make mistakes or struggle to learn how life is." Sandy continued, knowing full well that she was getting deeper into very dangerous territory. "I'm done with this conversation!" Alan said in a huff as he stormed out of Sandy's house.

The next morning at work, Sandy filled Jane in on what had happened. "Ooh, that's bad," Jane responded. "Yeah, he's been short with me the last few days. I really screwed up, but I just couldn't stop myself. I don't understand how he can stand to let his girls take advantage of him and his resources. At their ages, they should be helping him around the house, taking on responsibilities, getting jobs, and living on their own, but he doesn't make them do anything. It's so ridiculous!" Sandy complained.

"Not everyone parents the same way," Jane reasoned with her friend. "But I agree, it sounds like he could do or could have done much better at parenting. You're right; it's his responsibility to teach him the life skills they need, push them, and hold them accountable, but he hasn't done any of that. Maybe JoJo WAS right about staying far away from men with daughters." Said Jane. "I hope not because I think I'm in love with Alan, and I don't want to give up the possibility of a great relationship," Sandy said with a big sigh of frustration.

"You may need to choose between your relationship with Alan and needing to dispense your unsolicited parenting advice because you can't change him," Warned Jane. "I realized a long time ago that I can't change Dick, so I stopped

trying. Either drop it about his parenting and choose to be happy with him and who he is, or keep on the track you're going, and run the risk of it ending your relationship." "I don't like those options," huffed Sandy. "Well, like them or not, those are the only two options you have with Alan," Jane explained. She felt bad for Sandy. What a mess.

The issue you can run into with older children is that their behaviors and patterns have already been established, and it is usually very clear to them that you are not their parent. Many times, little kids have an easier time adjusting and accepting someone new, but older kids, not so much. If you find yourself in a situation of misaligned parenting styles combined with children who may not be receptive to a new partner, it can get bad as it did for Sandy.

If you find yourself disagreeing with how your partner is rearing their child, it's best to keep your mouth shut. Remember the adage: "If you don't have anything nice to say, don't say anything at all"? It 100% applies to this situation. If it helps to avoid bringing up that subject for you to stay neutral, then avoid it like the Ring-Around-the-Rosy plague!

Trying to change the way that your partner rears his or her child is like trying to get water to flow uphill. It's just not going to happen. In other words, we should all take my advice from the title of chapter six in my first book in The Suck Less Series: Chapter 6: Trying to Change Him Will Make You Miserable. And it will, indeed.

HER KIDS SAID

Mom: Do you remember the first time you met Andy?

Anthony: Yeah! Ish.

Cabbage: Yeah.

Mom: Describe what you remember that first meeting to have felt like.

Cabbage: Felt weird, that's for sure.

Anthony: I remember like, him coming to the house and then asking a lot of questions, and him saying his name and everything, and then his dog. That's pretty much all I remember. And I somehow still remember the wedding.

Mom: Do you remember how you felt when you met him because he was a stranger?

Cabbage: Weird.

Anthony: I felt excited.

Mom: Excited?

Anthony: Very.

Mom: Why?

Anthony: He looked COOL! (Raises arms out like he's flying)

Mom: (*Everyone laughing*) He looked cool?! That's funny. Cabbage, what do you remember?

Cabbage: Zero, but I don't know anything.

Mom: Cuz remember, there were all those Amy things, and you guys were playing together, and then the next morning… I have a picture of you looking at his tattoos, trying to figure out if they were permanently on his body.

Anthony: (*Mimicking Andy's voice*) Do pushups!

Cabbage: I don't remember.

Mom: Maybe you were too young. How do you see Andy now, in terms of a family member?

Cabbage: Awesome!

Anthony: He's a nice stepdad.

Cabbage: Yeah. He's like one of those fathers whom you rarely see.

Mom: What does that mean?

Anthony: You look up to.

Cabbage: Strong (*holds arms up*), nice…

Mom: Is it confusing to you that he isn't as strict or doesn't discipline like I do?

Cabbage: It's not weird.

Mom: Is it CONFUSING?

Cabbage: What do you mean, "confusing"?

Mom: Like, if I say, "You can't go in the mud puddle", and then I leave for work, and you're home with him, and he lets you go in the mud puddle, is that confusing to you?

Anthony: Well, yeah. Pretty confusing because you say "no", and he says "yes", but then if I defy whatever you say… yes, it's confusing.

Mom: Is it confusing to have a dad and an Andy?

Both: No.

Anthony: Not really, because we have a normal one and...

She: A normal what?

Anthony: A normal dad and an Andy.

Mom: What advice would you give to parents introducing another adult to their children?

Anthony: (Just throwing out answers so he can be done) Weird.

Mom: No, what advice would you give? Like if you saw this mom, and she was going to introduce her boyfriend to her kids, what would you tell her?

Cabbage: Tell the other parent?

Mom: Tell the other parent about the transition and that you're introducing someone to your children, is that what you mean?

Cabbage: What are you talking about?

Mom: Okay, so let's say it's a mom with a kid, and she's trying to introduce a new boyfriend to her kid, what advice would you give that mom about introducing him to her child?

Cabbage: (*Sighs because he's not understanding and wants it to be over.*)

Anthony: How do they do it in the movies? They say like here's somebody and somebody…

Mom: You don't think maybe they should wait until a certain amount of time, or maybe you should not force it…

Anthony: You should wait until whoever comes first, and then you can introduce them…

Mom: Okay, this is bad advice. What advice would you give to children of a divorce who are about to meet a parent's significant other?

Cabbage: I don't know (*has lost all interest in participating and has focused all attention on the cat*).

Anthony: You just have to deal with it, and say "This is your family"…

Mom: So, be nice to the new person and try to invite them into the family, and not be mean to them?

Both: Yeahhhhhh.

She: Is that it?

Both: Yeah. Pretty much.

Oof-Da. That was a painful interview to conduct and then to dictate. Trying to push your parenting agenda onto your new partner and his or her child is like backseat driving. How well does that usually work for you? It doesn't. Someone always freaks out.

Maybe the delicate dance of the stepchildren is more like when a cold front hits a warm front, a storm breaks out, and people die! If you are faced with the misaligned adult-children parenting nightmare, you only have two options.

1. Keep your unwanted opinions to yourself.

2. Dispense your advice and ruin the relationship you have with your partner.

I had to take MY advice, keeping my opinions to myself, for the sake of my very amazing relationship with the best husband ever. That meant avoiding topics that I knew would trigger unwanted advice. I saw no other way. I had to take the approach I take to saving money and avoiding my shopping trigger... just avoid and don't open emails from retailers I can't resist buying clothes or shoes from.

The best way to merge your family into a new, stronger unit is to communicate effectively with the children involved, have a conversation with your partner about what they would like their role to be in the parenting of your children or vice versa, and try to stay out of it when your advice isn't solicited. I know it's hard, but pushing your unsolicited agenda onto your partner will only stress you out and damage your relationship. Stay in your lane as much as possible and try to keep the overall health and happiness of the family unit in mind when you are dancing this delicate dance so you don't all fall down... and die!

Chapter 19:

When to Yank the Nest Out from Beneath Their Tiny Bird Feet

M.O.M. SAID

Some parents are coddlers, and some parents are kick-that-baby-bird-out-of-the-nest parents. Children of coddlers, or soft parents, will have a much harder time adjusting to life in the real world because the real world won't coddle them like they're used to. Their parents will have done them a big disservice by not pushing them to make their own mistakes and learn responsibility. I've got my boots ready for that swift kick when the time comes for me to bid my children adieu, but I am also actively teaching my children how to fly in preparation for the moment when I kick them out of the nest. Love you, BYEEEE!!!

There is a timeframe in parenting when children need to stay in the nest and be nurtured by the parents. Conversely, there is a time when as a parent, you need to trust that you've taught your children well and let them learn by making their own mistakes. Birds whose parents don't teach life skills will never leave the nest willingly and will struggle to fly and survive on their own. Shame on you, Coddle Birds. You're sucking a bit at parenting.

I was lucky to have been taken care of by my parents through college and then by my first husband right after I graduated, but I was deathly afraid of life on my own after college, which is why I planned my wedding to take place two weeks after I graduated. Anxiety riddled me in my last year of college because I hadn't had the chance to figure out many important life skills on my own. Yes, I had left the nest to attend college, but I had never really lived on my own with a full-time job and had to manage a house, bills, and vehicle on my own.

I was the youngest, and I'll admit that I was skilled at manipulation so some of that life naiveté is on me. Why did I manipulate my way into being taken care of? Because I could, because I was scared, because it was a survival tactic, and because it is in our nature to take the path of least resistance. How many of us would choose hardship if there was an option that avoided it?

It was nice to have been cared for seamlessly, but the downside was that it did not help me grow up, become independent, or learn to be a 100% responsible adult. Even after a decade of marriage, I still hadn't learned many independent life skills: budgeting, how to pump gas, how to mow the yard, how to use the snowblower, how to manage money, how to save for retirement, or how to deal with home repairs or broken appliances.

It wasn't until I got divorced and was living on my own with two children that I had to learn a lot of those critical life skills and learn them very quickly. Was it stressful? There was no more stressful time in my life! Do I wish that I had endured a little more hardship beforehand to teach me independence? Begrudgingly, yes.

Sandy's relationship with Alan and her little boys was going better than she could have imagined. When they were together, everything in the home just seemed to work better. The couple had made plans to move in together in a year, which gave them both time to sell their homes and to find one together.

"We need at least five bedrooms for our whole family, but we can't afford homes that big in the area we want to live in," explained a frustrated Sandy to Jane. "Why do you need that many bedrooms? Aren't his daughters old enough to be living on their own?" Jane asked, confused as much as her friend.

"Well, yeah, they are twenty and twenty-four now, but they don't seem very motivated to move out, and Alan isn't pushing them," she explained. "Well, if you can't afford a house that big, why doesn't he have a conversation with them about making plans to move out? They are adults, and they have a whole year. That should be more than enough time." Jane reasoned.

"Every time I bring it up to Alan, he shuts down. I love him so much, but he's a coddler... and an enabler. Plus, it's not my place; they aren't my kids." Sandy sighed. "But they are affecting your life and your family because they are using resources that they shouldn't be. Do they at least pay rent?" asked Jane, becoming as frustrated and annoyed as her friend.

"No. They only pay for their car insurance and cell phones, I think." Sandy said as she racked her brain for any other missing details. "Well, how does he expect his kids to know how to pay bills and manage their money if they have no lead-in to financial responsibility at home? Do they at least cook or clean or do anything to help him out?" Jane asked. "No. They play video games and hang out with their friends." Sandy sighed. "Honestly, you want to know something really bad?" She asked Jane. "Uh, what?"

"Every time he says he's going to hold his kids accountable for something but then he gives in, I lose a little bit of respect for him. Pretty soon, I'll have lost all respect for him, and then where will that leave our relationship?" asked a very

distressed Sandy. "Girl, that's a tough situation." Jane empathized. "If you love him as much as you say you do, you may just need to lay off him and let him figure it out on his own. As much as that sucks…" "Yeah. I love him, so I'll try to back off, but it's not going to be easy." Sandy resigned.

A few weeks later, after shopping for homes way outside their price range but that would accommodate the kids on both sides, Alan said to Sandy, "I think that it may be time for my girls to move out. They've lived with me well beyond where I should have let them. I'll talk to them both tomorrow about making plans." Having backed off and having let Alan come to his senses on his own saved Sandy from creating drama in their relationship and allowed Alan the time and space to arrive at the most logical conclusion.

It took a great deal of pushing and tough love as Alan's girls whined and protested, but they eventually figured out a way to make it work where they would share an apartment. "Alan, I think it was very brave of you and a big step in the right direction having your girls move out, and I'm so proud of you." Sandy praised as they moved into their new home. "It was really hard," Alan confessed, "Broke my heart a little, but you were right. I was coddling them too much and keeping them from starting to learn to live on their own. At least I figured it out before they were living in our basement with forty cats!" He joked. "Maybe we should leave the basement unfinished," Sandy jested as she kissed him and walked back outside to grab more boxes.

When most people become parents, they share the same mantras: "I want my children to have better than I had" or "I'm not going to make the same mistakes my parents made." We all enter parenthood with the best intentions, trying our darndest to keep our kids out of therapy when they get older. Parents coddle because they love their children, but after a certain point, coddling and enabling becomes a detriment, not an asset, to the development of children.

When is this magical changeover point at which we are supposed to stop coddling and enabling and start lacing up our boots to kick the baby birds out of the nest? I don't think that there's a magical time, but as your children get older, they should be given more responsibility and have more expectations placed upon them so that when they do leave, they aren't flailing, drowning, and running back to mom and dad's house.

Here are some rough guidelines that I have implemented and outlined to ease these transitions:

1. **Elementary School**

    a. Level 1 Chores: make the bed, put laundry away, clear dishes after meals, dry dishes, empty dishwasher, clean toilets, take the trash and recycling out, get the mail, wash the floors

    b. Level 1 Skills: help to bake (measuring, mixing, cracking eggs), vacuum

2. **Middle School**

    a. Level 2 Chores (in addition to level 1 chores): dust, other duties as assigned.

    b. Level 2 Skills: master cooking a simple meal while learning other cooking skills (browning burgers, making eggs, preheating and prepping pans, following recipes); learn to use the lawnmower; clean, organize, and purge bedroom, do laundry, learn money management (saving vs spending)

3. **High School**

    a. Level 3 Chores (in addition to level 1 and 2 chores): take initiative to pick up and help without being asked. Do all level 1 and 2 chores without being asked, snow blow the driveway, be responsible with a vehicle, take ownership of any costly mistakes with vehicle or otherwise (payment back plan or exchange of services), and shuttle younger siblings to and from events without incident.

b. Level 3 Skills: bake without help; plan, cook, and serve a meal; get and maintain a job, research and plan a path to a career

Children need to be given not only the skills and tools but also the confidence to try and make their own mistakes without having to rely on their parents anymore. For them to achieve this confidence, they need to be given more and more tasks and responsibilities with accountability so that they don't become overwhelmed when everything is tossed upon them all at once.

Confident children make confident and successful adults. The more prepared you can help them to be as they approach adulthood, the farther ahead they can leap when they do fly the nest. There may be points along their journey when you need to come alongside them to hold their hand and help them through, but if you do the work progressively, you will be able to stand back and watch them soar.

HER KIDS SAID

Mom: Let's try to do a little bit better.

Cabbage: I'm wiping the cat's butt.

Mom: Do you think kids today are being coddled or pushed to be independent?

Anthony: What does "coddled" mean?

Mom: It means babying them. Do you think most kids today are being babied or being pushed to be independent?

Anthony: I think the other one. Not being pushed, the other one.

Mom: Coddled. Cabbage (*playing slap battle with the cat*), can you pay attention? What do you think?

Cabbage: What Anthony said.

Mom: Why do you think that?

Cabbage: Because I don't want to say it.

Mom: Just say it.

Cabbage: I forgot. Wait, did he say "coddled"?

Mom: Okay, like when we get to school, and I say, "Anthony, get out, and walk to the door. I'm not pulling up to the front door." that's pushing you. Coddling is driving up to the front and waiting in line to do that so you can walk the shortest distance from the car to the school.

So, do you think most kids are being pushed or coddled?

Both: Coddled.

Mom: At what age do you think kids should know how to plan and cook a meal independently?

Cabbage: Ten, nine, or eight.

Anthony: Ten.

Mom: Ten?

Anthony: Ten-ish. Ten for cooking maybe, and what was the other one?

Mom: Cook and plan a meal by yourself.

Anthony: Oh, maybe eleven then.

Mom: So, in other words, you yourself have passed this mark, and you can't do it... is that what you're saying?

Anthony: What do you mean, "I can't do it"?

Mom: You haven't planned and cooked a meal by yourself.

Anthony: Yeah, oh. Well, let me think of an age. Maybe thirteen.

Mom: Thirteen? What do you think, Cabbage?

Cabbage: Twelve or ten because they should learn earlier.

Mom: You think... (*laughing*) You think, next year...

Cabbage: (*Getting defensive*) I'm not gonna know how to cook!

Mom: Okay, do you though?

Cabbage: No. Not by myself.

Mom: When I say "plan", I mean look at the recipe, plan out to get the ingredients, and then do all the whole meal by yourself.

Anthony: Thirteen-ish... fourteen.

Cabbage: Yeah.

Mom: Thirteen-fourteen? Okay. Do you feel like you will be prepared to live independently after graduating high school?

Anthony: Uuuuuuuhhhhhhhhh yeah. Pretty sure.

Cabbage: Yeah.

Anthony: Cuz wouldn't you be almost eighteen by then?

Mom: Yeah. Why or why not?

Anthony: Yeah, because you're eighteen.

Mom: Yes, but just because you're eighteen, that doesn't mean you have the life skills to live on your own. Why do you think that you WILL be able to live on your own…

Cabbage: (*Sucking both arms into his long-sleeve shirt and moving them around frantically*) Because I do a ton of chores for you! And because you teach me how to do things like start the dryer, clean the floors, clean the toilets, or restart the power, or… what's another one? Make my bed!

Mom: Anthony, what do you think?

Anthony: (*Groans*) You can live by yourself after high school because you have pretty much made it through the whole school year...

Mom: Yeah, but school and life are not the same thing.

Anthony: Yeah, I know.

Mom: What makes you specifically think that you will be ready to live on your own after you graduate?

Anthony: Oh, graduate from college?

Mom: High. School.

Anthony: Technically, can't your parents just tell you what and how to do things?

Mom: That's what the whole up-to-eighteen is for telling you and teaching you.

Anthony: Same thing.

Mom: Not really. What are you scared of when you think about living on your own?

Anthony: Things can happen more.

Mom: What does that mean?

Cabbage: Toilet overflow. I don't know how that would happen.

Anthony: Losing things.

Cabbage: That's for you. I don't lose things.

Mom: Are we concerned about paying bills…

Cabbage: I'm not worried…

Mom: Are we concerned about maintaining a vehicle?

Cabbage: Yeah, the vehicle part.

Anthony: Vehicle! Definitely, brah.

Cabbage: Because in some games I play, there's a ton of vehicles, and they show you what they can do. At school, we're learning about fossil fuels and the green future, and there was this story all about hybrid cars and electric cars, and people were for electric more than hybrid because electric doesn't use as.

Mom: What does that have to do with what you're scared of?

Cabbage: I don't know. Whatever. How much does a car cost?

Mom: Envision yourself moving out, living all by yourself…

Anthony: There's a lot more things…

Cabbage: Creepy things

Mom: What do you think would be intimidating and scary for you?

Cabbage: Someone knocking on the door at three AM. What would you do in that situation?

Mom: That's not what I mean.

Anthony: I don't know. Someone could break into your house when you're not there.

Mom: I'm talking about what you are scared of when managing your own life.

Cabbage: Oh. The furniture and where you want to put it. Where to go, and how expensive would your house and everything you want be? That's scary.

Anthony: Cuz what if you live a really far distance from work, and how are you supposed to remember that easily? There could be like road traffics.

Mom: So, we aren't concerned about doing our own laundry, keeping our house clean, making our own food, paying our own bills… any of those things. We aren't concerned about that?

Cabbage: I'm concerned about some of those.

Mom: Like which ones?

Cabbage: The bills, the cleaning, some other things you said.

Mom: You don't think that you'll have that figured out by the time you graduate?

Cabbage: I'll probably know those stuff.

Anthony: Probably the work you're going to have to do.

Mom: A job.

Anthony: Yeah. Because if you get like a job or something, you might have to work overnight and everything all the time… so that would suck.

Mom: (*Sighs heavily for getting pretty much nowhere and never being able to get those seven minutes back.*)

Parenting changes as your children go in and out of different phases of their lives. It is the parents' job to adapt their techniques to their children's ever-changing needs and aptitudes. We all know that life isn't easy so we need to control introducing them to increasingly harder challenges in an environment where we can still help teach our little ones how to manage life's hurdles.

Yes, there is a time and place for a degree of coddling. However, when children grow up, sheltering them from the outside world of swearing, violence, suicide, sex, and drugs (all the stuff rock and roll talks about) needs to shift to bring up these topics in an environment where they feel safe to express their feelings and have a real conversation. They should hear these things from you rather than be confronted with them at school or in a place where they have had no coaching in dealing with them.

If you don't slowly teach your baby birds how to fly out of the nest, and then all of a sudden the nest is yanked out from under their tiny bird feet, how well do you think that they will do on their own without the skills to fly, feed themselves, build their own nest, or survive in the wild on their own? I'm sorry, but if you were a bird parent, and your children were baby birds who weren't taught any life skills or responsibilities, your baby birds would be the ones who fall and flail, flap around on the ground, and then die a shriveled-up piece of cooked white meat in the sun. It'd be an ugly sight.

Chapter 20:

Be a Good Human

M.O.M. SAID

Most people's lives are crazy busy, and most don't take the time to look outside their circle or their lives to see where they can help others. Not everyone feels the calling to volunteer their time and resources on a board or at the local non-profit, but even if volunteering isn't your thing, it is your parental responsibility to find a way to teach your littles how to give back and that life is about more than their needs and wants.

Working at a non-profit, I am fortunate to get a lot of perspective on what life can give generously or take away suddenly, but even before taking this job, I felt like I needed to give back. One of the first things I did when I moved to Duluth was to join the Parent Teacher Organization (PTO). I remember heading off to the first meeting and my first husband saying, "Don't sign up for anything." I came back as the next elected President. Oops. Technically, I didn't sign up; I was voted in.

After my divorce, I started a charity. One of my hobbies is stress baking, and I bake in double or triple batches because it's more efficient. However, I bake like I fish… for sport. I love fishing, but I don't eat fish, and I love baking, but I don't eat what I make. One day, while on the treadmill at the gym, I had the best idea – to turn my passion for baking into something with a larger reach. The next day, my logo was designed, my website was up, my social media was live, and I had people reaching out to volunteer. The year of having that charity was one of the most fulfilling years of my life.

In my six years here in Duluth, I have found fulfillment in many additional long- and short-term volunteer opportunities in the community. Through these opportunities, I try to teach my children that it's important to give back and that there are two ways to do so: give money or give of your time and talent. I'm more of a time and talent kind of girl because I don't have the funds to give, but organizations need both to remain viable.

Recently, I spoke at a high school's service club meeting, and one of my talking points was how to suck less at volunteering. While the students in the room were volunteering their time to that organization's causes, I wanted to encourage and inspire them to continue giving back after graduation.

"How many of you are only in this club because it looks good on your college applications?" I asked pointedly. To my surprise, two students in the front row raised their hands. "Good for you for being honest!" I laughed. "How many of you think that you will volunteer after your lives are filled with a family and a career?" About two-thirds of the room raised their hands, but they were unsure when I asked what they were passionate about volunteering to do or volunteer for.

"Volunteering is something you'll only do if you are passionate about the cause. That could be volunteering at the animal shelter as a cat cuddler. There is a disconnect between this generation and service clubs like this and translating that spirit of giving back to life in your twenties and beyond," I noted. My goal was to plant seeds of introspective thought that they might remember someday when their lives move past high school. Hopefully, some of them will want to continue to suck less at giving back and will change the world for the better.

I hope my children will inherit my drive to make a difference when they grow up. Being an active member of multiple non-profits, I see the number of volunteers consistently dwindling. People don't come to meetings for fear of being guilted into something. Service clubs used to be packed with leaders from the community, and now it's mostly retirees and the few people who are simply compelled to volunteer.

One of my friends who volunteers alongside me said that her husband isn't very supportive of how much she volunteers because she's never home. I know I complain when it's time to go back to the school to run the PTO meetings at night, but that's because I'm a morning person, and I'm 90% zombie by the time the six pm meeting starts. Regardless, having a spouse who doesn't support your good deeds only makes the saying, "No good deed goes unpunished," even truer.

If you're not one of those who are called to volunteer, then at least you should support the people who are. While my husband is glad that my PTO time is ending, the man is a public servant in his 9-5… or 7-5. Just last evening, I was talking to him on his drive back to his house from work, and he said he needed to stop at the store on his way home.

"Didn't you just go to the store yesterday?" I asked. "Yes, but there's this homeless couple that I keep running into when I have to clear out the homeless camps. They have nothing. I asked them what their shoe sizes were and told them I would buy them boots. They don't look like they will survive long in this cold without them." My husband is no saint, and he and I are both admittedly selfish to a degree, but it's in instances like that where I find reaffirmation of why I love him. He's a cop, he's not rich, but he has the heart of a warrior who lives with honor, and that's a great example to set.

Dick and Jane were regular volunteers at their local soup kitchen. Every Sunday, their little family would head out to help serve in the lunch line. "Mom," Joy started, "Poppy said that her mom said that homeless people should just get a job and should stop being a burden to society. What does that mean?" she asked her mother.

Taking a moment to think, Jane responded, "Well honey, unfortunately, some people share that sentiment that homeless people are using taxpayer money as an excuse not to work, but it's so much more complicated than that. Sometimes, people struggle with mental illness or struggle to break the cycle of poverty in their families. Maybe you should invite Poppy with us one Sunday," Jane offered.

"Okay!" Said Joy as she immediately pulled out her phone to text Poppy. "That sounds awful. Why would you want to spend your weekend with homeless people?" Poppy replied. "What am I

supposed to say to that?" Joy asked her parents. "Tell her that we really enjoy it and that we will take her for ice cream after," Dick said. Poppy reluctantly agreed, and the next Sunday, the four of them donned their logoed aprons and stood at their stations in the lunch line.

A mother with a three-year-old little girl came up to Poppy's station in line. "Hi. What's your name?" Poppy tried. "Annie. Thank you for the food. I haven't eaten since yesterday," she said as her eyes never left the ground. "Oh... I'm sorry," replied Poppy, struggling with what to say. "Have a good day!" she added awkwardly as the pair moved down the line.

After the lunch line closed, Poppy started crying as she was helping clean up. "What's the matter?" Joy asked her friend. "That little girl... she said she hadn't eaten since yesterday. It's so sad. I didn't understand what you were talking about when you said you enjoyed helping out here. I wish that I could do more for that family," she admitted.

"The good thing is that you can, Poppy. You can come back here and volunteer or see if the people

here know if that family needs anything in particular. Maybe you could collect some items to donate. There are always ways to help people," Jane explained, stepping into the conversation.

"I will! I'll talk to my parents. I want to help more people!" Poppy exclaimed as her newfound humility began to inspire her to action.

There's so much to being a good person that I want my children to go out into the world with, and one of those such things is giving love to people who don't have enough of it. When I worked in senior care, I saw so many seniors sit alone every day with no visits from family or friends. It's heartbreaking to witness the sad, quiet of loneliness day after day. When I was about to leave senior care for a new job, I felt torn about the friends I was leaving behind. Surely, there wasn't a way to take them all with me, but not taking any just didn't feel right.

After a few restless nights thinking over what to do, I decided to adopt a senior named Nancy. Ironically, that's my mom's name, so we made up the name "GG" for great Grandma. My

Grandparents were all gone, and most of her family had passed. She'd lost a husband, daughters, and grandchildren... more loss of immediate family than one person should have to bear. Truth be told, her enthusiasm to help and do projects had at one point become taxing on my staff in the Life Enrichment department. They asked me to speak with her, and in doing so, I made a friend. (Ironically, she has now become an invaluable volunteer asset to the Life Enrichment department.)

She comes over to my house about once a month for a home-cooked meal, a glass of sweet, bubbly wine, and some honest girl talk. My wedding to Andy was intimately small with under twenty attendees, and she was one of them because she's family, our my adopt-a-Grandparent. My children have welcomed her as a member of our family because they have witnessed me do just that. Sometimes, I find it hard to fit in time to see her, but every time I do, I'm so glad that I did.

The whole circumstance makes me wonder why more people don't adopt a senior. Honestly, that's where my "suck less" saying originates. *"If everyone just sucked a little less, the world would be a much better place."* I say it so often that my bestie gave me a gift of a sparkly pink compact engraved with "Suck Less" on the back! In all seriousness, everyone can change the world by changing one person's life. In changing one person's life, you have changed their world, and isn't that something that we should try to pass along to the next generation?

I'm as busy as a person can be, but I make time for things and people that are important. My hope for my children is that they become good humans, people who are kind, empathetic, and passionate about a cause, so much so that they are willing to give up their time, talent, and resources. Why? Because when we're gone, what kind of legacy do we want to leave? Jobs are jobs, things are just things, money is just money, but impacting the lives of others can last forever. I just want to make a difference, and teaching my children to be altruistic is my way of ensuring that I pass along the passion of giving back.

HER KIDS SAID

Mom: Last one. Try your hardest! Do you know what Mommy does at work?

Cabbage: (*Raises his hand*) Um, help people who are in need of food, water, shelter, space…

Anthony: What? Space?

Cabbage: And then people who are poor come in, and then you give them free food or water or something like that.

Mom: Anthony?

Anthony: Yeah, same thing.

Mom: Do you feel like GG is a part of our family? Why?

Cabbage: Kinda.

Anthony: Kind of.

Mom: Why?

Anthony: Well, she has only been with us for a year…

Cabbage: She's not Asian!

Mom: Neither is Daddy… Neither is Andy. Somebody doesn't need to be Asian to be part of the family. Concentrate – this is the last one. Do you think that when you grow up, you will want to volunteer to help others?

Anthony: In certain ways.

Mom: Volunteering means that you aren't getting paid for it.

Both: Yes!

Mom: What would you like to volunteer to do?

Cabbage: I don't know. I forgot.

Mom: Okay, I volunteer as the Parent Teacher Organization President, I'm also the Vice President for another organization.

Cabbage: Remember those questions before about what do you want to do for a tradition or something?

Mom: Yeah.

Cabbage: Um, make cookies, and give 'em away.

Mom: Oh, who else did that?

Cabbage: (*Points at me*)

Mom: That's right. But volunteering means that you go and help other organizations that are already helping people, you know, because they need volunteers to do things because they don't usually make a lot of money, so people volunteer their time so they don't have to pay someone to do that thing.

Anthony: Probably just help my neighbor do stuff if they're nice.

Cabbage: Yeah.

Anthony: Yard work.

Mom: What do you think it means to be a good person?

Anthony: Help people with stuff that they didn't even ask you to help with.

Cabbage: (*Raising his hand*) Ooh, ooh! Be nice. Don't ask just do it. Um, be kind. Be helpful. Don't be angry at them if they mess up something. Be polite. Don't get into fights and other stuff.

Anthony: Well, and also say like, "Do you need help with that?"

If you want your children to be good people, you will need to lead by example. Yes, some people find their way to altruism or philanthropy because of experiences they have had in their lives, but if more parents taught their children to give back, we could change the world. There are innumerable causes and non-profits out there in every community that are desperate for volunteers or members to help join them in their causes.

Most organizations don't even need volunteers for many hours a month. I'd say the average involvement of an active volunteer is about four hours a month. Don't you think that your child's perspective on the world is worth four hours a month? If I didn't HAVE to work, I would love to write books and volunteer. You will always get more out of volunteering and giving back than you put in. Always. It's a gift that you can give your children that they can give back to the world.

Chapter 21:

Monsters Be Gone

M.O.M. SAID

Wouldn't it be wonderful if there was a spray called "Monsters Be Gone" that you could just spray your children with, and they would turn into perfect angels? Sorry, Amazon hasn't come out with it yet. But there are ways in which you can prevent your littles from growing up and into their monster horns, and I hope that you will have learned some of those techniques from my experiences and advice.

I'll be the first to admit that I am not a perfect parent. No one is. The best we can do as parents is to try our hardest every day to set an example for who we want our children to become. We all see our parents in ourselves, and our children will be no different. Will there be days that we just make mistake after mistake, only to live with growing parent guilt at the end of the day? Of course. The only thing you can do when you have a day like that is to try harder the next day because your children are always watching and listening, and they will emulate what you do, not what you tell them to do.

Entertaining the idea of becoming a parent is like the start of the new year. Everyone makes resolutions to do better at this or that or to check things off a bucket list. That kind of forward-looking drive and optimism toward a better you should be a mindset that you carry throughout your journey of parenthood. If you're not moving forward, you're not learning or growing, and neither will your children. Every parent's failure can be the end of the old year, and the next morning can be the start of the new year for resolutions to begin. As long as you keep trying to move the needle forward to a better you, you are being a good parent.

As a parent, it is your job to establish yourself as the boss. You are the supervisor, the CEO, the President of your family, and the Manager of Monsters (M.O.M.). You need to establish the rules with your team, enforce the rules, write up behavior correction plans, schedule appropriate training, and maintain authority. In your role as CEO of your family, you should demand respect, but that respect needs to be earned first.

Imagine if, at work, your boss was more interested in having her employees like her and be her friends than she was interested in establishing boundaries and establishing herself as the authority figure of the group. What do you think those team meetings would look like? Would they be structured, on time, and run professionally? No. They would be a hot disaster! Furthermore, her employees wouldn't treat her with the respect that a workplace boss deserves. Her employees would act like little monsters who communicated disrespectfully, whined for what they wanted, and she would give in. This type of boss is ineffective and a bad leader... a soft parent. It is a lot easier to understand the correct role of parents when you put it in a less emotional scenario like work.

Parenting is a job that you don't get paid for. If there were no guidelines, schedules, or a routine of any kind, imagine how difficult your job would be. Try to see your children's perspective from their employee standpoint, and work on creating processes and procedures that will put everyone in the family on the same path to success. Remember, you are also trying to teach your children how to manage their time effectively, how to plan, and how to be respectful. You're the boss, the head honcho, so act like it and suck less.

One of the biggest keys to success in parenting is consistency. Whatever rules you make, whatever boundaries you set, whatever punishment or reward systems you roll out, consistency is the determining factor that will make it successful. Fight through the tired, fight through the distractions, fight through the stress of life to maintain your consistency, and I guarantee you, it will pay off.

While being a parent is one of the hardest roles in life that you will ever play, you must also find the fun in it. If that means making up a quirky version of the Tooth Fairy or lying about too much sugar causing the squirts, you must laugh and you must enjoy your children for as long as you have them. One of the greatest things I've learned from adopting GG into our family is that just because you are a parent, you are not guaranteed to outlive your children or your grandchildren. Find some of that wisdom in your life and cherish those little people who drive you insane. Nothing in life is a guarantee, and looking back on a life with regrets is a deep sadness you can change and avoid right now.

Makeup traditions, take those family road trips, learn a new skill together, go for adventures outside, and find ways to connect with your children even if they roll their eyes at it. It's those experiences and those memories that they will cherish as they leave the nest and start their own lives.

Try your hardest to impart upon them the life skills that you've mastered, and learn together the ones that you all can do better at. Life is about learning, and parenting is about teaching. Prepare your children as best as you can to be able to be confident in their life skills as they make their way in the world.

Don't hide your struggles from your children. Use life's many teachable moments to talk to your children about processing emotions, about hardships, about overcoming adversity, and about doing the right thing even if no one is looking. There is no better teacher than life itself, and in those moments of stark reality, they will have a better understanding of the lessons you are trying to teach because of the real emotions they experience through you.

Most importantly, become a better human so that you can lead by example how to be compassionate and empathetic toward others. Volunteer together, adopt a family at Christmas, or adopt a lonely senior. Your family will bond on a deeper level that you may not come to understand fully for years to come, but when you do, you'll know you didn't suck at parenting.

What is the benchmark of success in parenting? How and when do you know that you sucked less as a parent? You'll know in little moments along the journey: in the time your child was late to be picked up because he was helping a student in a wheelchair with her books, in the little notes left outside your bedroom door that say "I love you", in the initiative to help without being asked, in the kindness they show others, in the laughter you share, in the memories you make, and in the hugs that you cherish.

Parenting is a gift, one that doesn't always come easily to some. Sure, it's hard, and it sucks sometimes, but don't beat yourself up too much when you find yourself sucking. We all do it, and our kids won't likely need therapy for each time that we suck at parenting. Hopefully.

> Truth be told, parenting is a journey of discovery and growth for the parents and the children. Some days, the parents will be the teachers and some days, the children will be the teachers. Both parties simply need to be willing to learn from each other, try their hardest to be better than their last mistake, and move forward with an unconditional love that only the ones we call "family" can share.

Bibliography

Helplama. 2023. "Beauty Industry Revenue and Usage Statistics 2023." Helplama.com. July 3, 2023. https://helplama.com/beauty-industry-revenue-usage-statistics/.

"Skincare Market." n.d. Allied Market Research. Accessed December 22, 2023. https://www.alliedmarketresearch.com/skincare-market-A31878.

Cyndi Lewis was born in South Korea, was adopted to Wisconsin, and currently lives in Duluth, MN. Her decades of writing marketing copy, blogs, press releases, magazine articles, and short stories have sharpened her writing skills. Lewis is passionate about advising on subjects that she is successful in hopes of helping as many people as possible find love, hope, happiness, and fulfillment.

Written in less than a year and all releasing in 2024, The Suck Less Series is a memoir-based advice trilogy that is funny, relatable, and empowering.

Book #1: Suck Less at Love: She Said, He Said Advice on Relationships

Book #2: Suck Less at Parenting: How NOT to Raise Little Monsters

Book #3: Suck Less at Life: Defy Mediocrity & Live without Regrets

Follow Lewis' author profile on
http://Amazon.com and
Instagram: (@cyndilewisauthor)
for updates on her new releases.
http://www.CyndiLewisAuthor.com

www.ingramcontent.com/pod-product-compliance
Lightning Source LLC
Chambersburg PA
CBHW070459120526
44590CB00013B/690